BEST-LOVED
MAIN COURSES
FOR SPECIAL OCCASIONS

BEST-LOVED

Discover the world's classic dishes in this fully
illustrated cook's guide to effortless entertaining

MAIN COURSES
FOR SPECIAL OCCASIONS

85 wonderful recipes shown with over 380 step-by-step photographs

Jenni Fleetwood

southwater

This edition is published by Southwater

Southwater is an imprint of Anness Publishing Ltd
Hermes House, 88–89 Blackfriars Road, London SE1 8HA
tel. 020 7401 2077; fax 020 7633 9499

www.southwaterbooks.com; www.annesspublishing.com

If you like the images in this book and would like to investigate using them for publishing,
promotions or advertising, please visit our website www.practicalpictures.com for more information.

UK agent: The Manning Partnership Ltd, 6 The Old Dairy, Melcombe Road, Bath BA2 3LR
tel. 01225 478444; fax 01225 478440; sales@manning-partnership.co.uk

UK distributor: Grantham Book Services Ltd
Isaac Newton Way, Alma Park Industrial Estate, Grantham, Lincs NG31 9SD
tel. 01476 541080; fax 01476 541061; orders@gbs.tbs-ltd.co.uk

North American agent/distributor: National Book Network
4501 Forbes Boulevard, Suite 200, Lanham, MD 20706
tel. 301 459 3366; fax 301 429 5746; www.nbnbooks.com

Australian agent/distributor: Pan Macmillan Australia
Level 18, St Martins Tower, 31 Market St, Sydney, NSW 2000
tel. 1300 135 113; fax 1300 135 103; customer.service@macmillan.com.au

New Zealand agent/distributor: David Bateman Ltd
30 Tarndale Grove, Off Bush Road, Albany, Auckland
tel. (09) 415 7664; fax (09) 415 8892

Previously published as part of a larger volume, *Classic Main Course Dishes*

Publisher: Joanna Lorenz
Editorial Director: Helen Sudell
Editors: Joy Wotton and Elizabeth Woodland
Production Controller: Wendy Lawson
Designers: Nigel Partridge, Steers McGillan Ltd and Sarah Williams
Cover Designer: Balley Design Associates
Recipes: Alex Barker, Carla Capalbo, Lesley Chamberlain, Jacqueline Clark, Roz Denny,
Patrizia Diemling, Matthew Drennan, Joanna Farrow, Valerie Ferguson, Jenni Fleetwood,
Silvano Franco, Yasuko Fukuoka, Shirley Gill, Brian Glover, Nicola Graimes, Juliet Harbutt,
Deh-Ta Hsiung, Christine Ingram, Manisha Kanani, Emi Kasuko, Lucy Knox, Gilly Love,
Lesley Mackley, Norma MacMillan, Jane Milton, Sallie Morris, Anne Sheasby, Marlena Spieler,
Linda Tubby, Laura Washburn and Kate Whiteman
Photographers: Nicki Dowey, Michelle Garrett, Amanda Heywood, Janine Hosegood, David Jordan,
Dave King, William Lingwood, Thomas Odulate, Craig Robertson and Sam Stowell

10 9 8 7 6 5 4 3 2 1

NOTES
Bracketed terms are intended for American readers.

For all recipes, quantities are given in both metric and imperial measures and, where
appropriate, in standard cups and spoons. Follow one set, but not a mixture, because they
are not interchangeable.

Standard spoon and cup measures are level. 1 tsp = 5ml, 1 tbsp = 15ml, 1 cup = 250ml/8fl oz.

Australian standard tablespoons are 20ml. Australian readers should use 3 tsp in place of 1 tbsp
for measuring small quantities of gelatine, flour, salt, etc.

American pints are 16fl oz/2 cups. American readers should use 20fl oz/2.5 cups in place of
1 pint when measuring liquids.

Electric oven temperatures in this book are for conventional ovens. When using a fan oven, the
temperature will probably need to be reduced by about 10–20°C/20–40°F. Since ovens vary, you
should check with your manufacturer's instruction book for guidance.

The nutritional analysis given for each recipe is calculated per portion (i.e. serving or item),
unless otherwise stated. If the recipe gives a range, such as Serves 4–6, then the nutritional
analysis will be for the smaller portion size, i.e. 6 servings. Measurements for sodium do not
include salt added to taste.

Medium (US large) eggs are used unless otherwise stated.

Front cover shows chicken marinated in maple and lemon – for recipe, see page 72.

CONTENTS

INTRODUCTION

Fifty years ago, main dishes were just that – the most important part of any meal and the course around which all others revolved. Most cookbooks of that era focused on the roast, the casserole or the mixed grill, paying scant attention to any other dishes. Then came the food revolution. People started eating out more and, as they dwelt on the delights of appetizers and desserts, main dishes started to take second place. In some restaurants, main courses disappeared entirely. Now it appears as though the pendulum has swung again. Nostalgia, coupled with nutritional advice that stresses the importance of eating small amounts of protein with plenty of vegetables, has put the main course back where it rightfully belongs – as the pivotal part of every meal.

However, the main course still has something of an image problem. Appetizers and desserts are seen as enticing and exciting, but main courses seem to have earned adjectives like "comforting", "robust", "satisfying" and "rib-sticking". When it comes to planning a special occasion meal, most of us have no difficulty in deciding what to serve for the first and final courses – it's what comes between the first and the last that proves to be the most problematic.

That's where this book comes in. With over 85 recipes you need never struggle for inspiration again. In fact, the difficulty will lie in deciding what to choose from this superb collection, whether it be a colourful healthy salad, a stunning soufflé, a pasta dish or the full works in the form of a meat or chicken roast or a hearty casserole.

BREAKING THE RULES

The days of the marathon meal – with an appetizer or soup leading to the fish course, followed by a meat dish, a sorbet, dessert, crackers and cheese and, finally, coffee – have largely disappeared. And today it is perfectly acceptable simply to serve guests a satisfying stew with lots of deliciously crusty bread for mopping up the juices, a beautiful baked fish with a pile of buttery new potatoes or a home-baked pie with a crisp salad. The rule is that there are virtually no rules, so that when you are entertaining at home, you can dispense with soups and appetizers altogether, if you like, or you can simply offer guests canapés with their drinks as they arrive.

The classic meat-and-two-veg theme has also vanished as more people have either become vegetarians or simply chosen to limit the amount of meat they eat. Today, a main course can be a roulade, a pie, a risotto, a substantial soup – or anything else you choose to serve. Thai-style spicy salad with warm, thinly sliced beef would go down well, as would a home-made pizza with a fresh spinach and egg topping. A simple cheese soufflé, perhaps with a salad or steamed vegetables, is always popular; and roasted vegetables, such as squash with a vegetarian stuffing of rice, goat's cheese, olives and sun-dried tomatoes, can make an unusual and impressive meal.

You don't necessarily have to serve vegetables alongside your chosen main dish either. Instead, they can star in the appetizer or appear in a salad, served French-style as a separate course. When serving vegetables, consider a fresh medley of steamed batons of carrots, leeks and celery, for instance, or a mixture of roast vegetables. That way you cut down on last-minute cooking, and avoid the flurry in the kitchen when your guests have just arrived. You'll have time to make them welcome.

Although the rules may have been relaxed somewhat, some of the old traditions remain intact, simply because they make good sense. Whatever you choose to serve, the meal should always

Left: A filling risotto made with fresh seafood is an elegant and delicious alternative to a traditional meat-and-two-vegetable main meal.

Above: Beautifully presented and elegantly garnished food will always be more appetizing.

Below: Casseroles, stews and curries are best served as a main course when they are not preceded by soups.

be balanced in terms of flavours, colours and textures. For example, it wouldn't be a good idea to serve a creamy mousse as a main course then follow it with a silky-smooth dessert, or to serve a juicy Thai stew or curry after a soup. If the main course is quite dry, for example a country meat loaf, it should be accompanied by a succulent side dish, such as creamed leeks or mushrooms. It also makes good sense to try and avoid using the same ingredients in successive courses as repeatedly encountering the same flavours and textures can be boring.

THE FINER DETAILS

The appearance of the food on the plate has become almost as important as the actual taste, so do give some thought to the colours and shapes of the ingredients used in the dish. Although the ubiquitous sprig of parsley seems to have been consigned to the great herb garden in the sky, more

interesting garnishes, such as tiny bunches of redcurrants, braided chives or cucumber ribbons can add colour and shape to any plate. Just make sure the garnish is appropriate – try lemon wedges with a fish dish, a fresh sprig of herbs on a vegetable stew, or spring onion curls with an Asian curry.

STRESS-FREE COOKING

When planning any meal, make life easy for yourself by preparing or cooking as much as possible ahead of time. Ease a heavy workload by using kitchen appliances such as the microwave oven, food processor and any other time-saving equipment you may have. Make use of your refrigerator and freezer – many dishes are even better when made ahead of time and reheated.

Most importantly, enjoy yourself – cooking and sharing good food with friends and family is one of life's greatest pleasures, so master these main dishes and you'll have many wonderful meals in store.

CHOOSING ACCOMPANIMENTS

The decision about what side dishes to serve with your chosen main dish will depend very much on whatever else is on the menu. You don't have to serve a vast array of vegetable accompaniments, especially if you've started the meal with a salad or a fruit appetizer, such as grapefruit cocktail or a slice of melon. It is, however, traditional (and sound nutritional sense) to offer a carbohydrate of some sort alongside the main dish. Obvious choices would be rice, potatoes, pasta and bread, but you could also choose grains such as couscous, polenta and lentils or even quinoa (pronounced keen-wa), an extremely nutritious and tasty South American grain, that is cooked in a similar way to rice.

RICE

If you choose rice, make sure that it complements the main course. Basmati rice, with its slightly nutty flavour, is perfect for Indian dishes, whereas Thai fragrant rice is the first choice for a green or red curry from that country. Try to experiment with the more unusual rices, too, such as the red rice from the Camargue and California. Brown rice makes a good accompaniment to vegetable casseroles and stews, or it can be cooked, cooled and made into a salad to serve with kebabs and grilled meat.

POTATOES

Mashed or creamed potato tastes great with creamy fish dishes, fried liver and sausages and pork casserole. The modern trend is to flavour the mash with garlic, mustard or herbs. You could try a mixture of mashed potato and celeriac, or mashed potato and swede (rutabaga). Sweet potato mash tastes great, too – for extra interest, stir in a few spoonfuls of a hot Mexican tomato salsa. For smooth results, use a ricer, potato masher or fork.

Roast potatoes and baked layered potatoes are great served with roasts, baked fish or pot roasts, while potato chips (French fries) or fried potatoes are often partnered with steak.

Baked potatoes, split and topped with butter, cream cheese, Stilton or crème fraîche are delicious with grills (broils). When the first new potatoes arrive in the shops, they are a special treat, especially if you toss the boiled or steamed potatoes with butter and chopped fresh parsley or finely grated lemon rind. For flap-free main courses, consider potato dishes that don't require any last-minute attention.

GRAINS AND PULSES

Couscous is an excellent partner for Moroccan tagines and similar dishes that have quite a lot of liquid. It is readily available from supermarkets and the latest pre-cooked forms of couscous are exceptionally quick and easy to prepare. Polenta is an Italian staple and is a very good alternative to mashed potato. Soft polenta can be served with stews and casseroles and when polenta is grilled, it is an excellent alternative to bread. Quinoa, which is available from health food stores, is a nutty-flavoured grain that goes well with vegetable stews, such as ratatouille, and bean pots. Although lentils are usually included as an ingredient in a recipe, Puy lentils are a classic French accompaniment. Serve them hot with braised meat and game.

Left: Mashed potato is a versatile accompaniment, whether served plain or flavoured with herbs or mustard.

Above: Serve piping-hot garlic bread with baked pasta dishes.

PASTA

There are many different forms of pasta, from Italian spaghetti and tagliatelle to the wide range of Asian egg and rice noodles. Choose the type that suits your dish, not just in terms of its origin, but also to reap maximum value from the shape. Slim or flat noodles are not only great with thin, creamy sauces, they also go well with stir-fried vegetables, while penne and rigatoni are sturdy enough for chunky sauces.

BREAD

If you are serving a rich casserole or stew that has plenty of gravy or sauce, a rustic loaf or a supply of freshly baked wholemeal (whole-wheat) rolls will not only suit the mood of the meal, but also give guests an excuse to mop up every last drop of gravy. There are dozens of delicious loaves available, so try some unusual varieties. Soda bread is perfect with an Irish stew, while lavash, a large flat bread that is torn into pieces at the table, is great with Middle Eastern dishes. Italian breads, such as focaccia, are ideal with hearty casseroles such as osso bucco. Garlic bread is delicious with fish brochettes, grilled (broiled) pork chops or lamb steaks cooked on the barbecue. For a change, make your own garlic butter and transform rolls into individual garlic and herb breads.

SALADS

Although substantial salads, such as Peruvian Salad or Thai Beef Salad, make perfect main course dishes in their own right, those salads that are less elaborate and substantial are better served as accompaniments to main meals. Use really fresh ingredients as these have a far superior flavour and crisp texture.

Salads don't work particularly well with meat or chicken stews or very creamy dishes, but they are perfect partners for pizzas, cold pies, baked pasta dishes such as lasagne, roulades, fajitas and grilled (broiled) fish and meat dishes. A simple green salad tossed with fresh herbs picked from the garden or window box is ideal and not overly time-consuming to make. Salads based on tomatoes, with added ingredients such as red onion or orange segments, are not only versatile but also simple to prepare.

Salad dressings should be kept simple so as not to compete with the other flavours in the bowl. A mixture of lemon juice, olive oil, fresh herbs, salt and freshly ground black pepper proves ideal for most salads and takes minutes to prepare, and any dressing that you don't use can be stored in the refrigerator until needed.

Below: A crisp salad is easy to prepare and goes well with main courses that don't contain a lot of sauce.

VEGETABLES

The choice of which vegetables to serve as accompaniments depends on what is part of the main dish. A main dish that includes a selection of vegetables, such as escalopes of chicken with baby vegetables, would be good on its own, or with potatoes or a similar starchy vegetable. However, you might wish to offer a selection of three or four different vegetables with roast lamb or pork. Try to balance crisp vegetables such as roast potatoes, lightly cooked broccoli and crunchy cabbage with creamy offerings such as puréed celeriac, carrot or parsnip.

Always imagine what the food will look like on the plate and aim to have a mixture of colours and textures. For example, baby carrots, puréed spinach and fried potatoes would add colour as well as texture to a main course, whereas mashed potato, cauliflower and braised celery would look – and taste – rather plain and dreary.

CONDIMENTS AND SAUCES

Many dishes are enhanced if they are served with a complementary relish or sauce. Roasts are traditionally served with rich-flavoured sauces: cranberry sauce with turkey, mint sauce with lamb and horseradish cream with beef. Spicy

Below: Braised leeks make a wonderful accompaniment when teamed with sweet carrots.

food is best with a cooling condiment. Curry, for instance, is complemented by a cucumber raita. When serving chilli dishes, piquant relishes and tomato salsas are perfect, adding colour and texture to the meal. Classic Italian salsa verde is a natural partner for sautéed fish or grilled steak, while a rich onion gravy goes well with sausages, liver, pork chops or toad-in-the-hole. Dark rich gravies are also good with mounds of creamy mashed potato.

Classic vegetable companions
Some vegetables seem to go particularly well with specific meat, poultry or fish dishes.
• The slightly tart flavour of braised red cabbage with apples is excellent with roast pork or baked ham.
• Fennel, with its delicate, almost aniseedy flavour, is the perfect partner for fish or chicken.
• Sweet-tasting corn and smoked haddock go well together, but it is better to use naturally-coloured haddock to avoid overdoing the yellow theme.
• Mashed swede (rutabaga) is the classic accompaniment for haggis, but also tastes great with herbed sausages or spicy minced (ground) beef patties.
• Spinach is classically served with veal dishes and it also goes well with fish dishes.
• Sweet potatoes, especially when candied, are simply superb with baked ham. They are also the classic accompaniment for Thanksgiving turkey.
• Green beans frequently partner tomato-based stews, but they are also very good with grilled meats and fish.
• Roast vegetables, such as aubergines (eggplant), red onion, courgettes (zucchini) and celery, make a colourful bed for baked chicken breast portions or pork chops, and are also excellent with roast meats of all types.

SOUPS AND SALADS

Nothing is more comfortingly satisfying than a bowl of steaming soup on a chilly evening, while a flavoursome, crunchy salad would be equally welcome for an al fresco *summer lunch. Any one of the dishes in this chapter is sure to impress and delight your guests, whether you choose a classic Bouillabaisse, spicy Seafood Laksa, or exotic Chicken and Mango Salad.*

MATELOTE

TRADITIONALLY THIS FISHERMEN'S SOUP IS MADE FROM FRESHWATER FISH, INCLUDING EEL, ALTHOUGH IN NORMANDY, THEY USE SEA FISH AND CONGER EEL. ANY FIRM FISH CAN BE USED, BUT TRY TO INCLUDE AT LEAST SOME EEL, AND USE A ROBUST DRY WHITE OR RED WINE FOR EXTRA FLAVOUR.

SERVES SIX

INGREDIENTS

1kg/2¼lb mixed fish, including
   450g/1lb conger eel if possible
50g/2oz/¼ cup butter
1 onion, thickly sliced
2 celery sticks, thickly sliced
2 carrots, thickly sliced
1 bottle dry white or red wine
1 fresh bouquet garni containing
   parsley, bay leaf and chervil
2 cloves
6 black peppercorns
beurre manié for thickening
   (see Cook's Tip)
salt and cayenne pepper
For the garnish
   25g/1oz/2 tbsp butter
   12 baby (pearl) onions, peeled
   12 button (white) mushrooms
   chopped flat leaf parsley

1 Cut all the fish into thick slices, removing any obvious bones. Melt the butter in a large pan, add the fish and sliced vegetables and stir over a medium heat until lightly browned. Pour in the wine and enough cold water to cover. Add the bouquet garni and spices and season. Bring to the boil, lower the heat and simmer gently for 20–30 minutes, until the fish is tender, skimming the surface occasionally.

2 Meanwhile, prepare the garnish. Heat the butter in a deep frying pan and sauté the baby onions until golden and tender. Add the mushrooms and cook until golden. Season and keep hot.

3 Strain the soup through a large sieve placed over a clean pan. Discard the herbs and spices in the sieve, then divide the fish among deep soup plates (you can skin the fish if you wish, but this is not essential) and keep hot.

4 Reheat the soup until it boils. Lower the heat and whisk in the *beurre manié* little by little until the soup thickens. Season to taste with salt and pepper and pour over the fish. Garnish each portion with the sautéed baby onions and mushrooms and sprinkle with chopped parsley. Serve immediately.

COOK'S TIP
To make the *beurre manié* for thickening, mix 15g/½oz/1 tbsp softened butter with 15ml/1 tbsp plain (all-purpose) flour. Add to the boiling soup, a pinch at a time, whisking constantly.

Per portion: Energy 305Kcal/1275kJ; Protein 32.1g; Carbohydrate 5.7g, of which sugars 4.6g; Fat 8.4g, of which saturates 4.6g; Cholesterol 94mg; Calcium 49mg; Fibre 1.6g; Sodium 169mg.

PROVENÇAL FISH SOUP

THE RICE MAKES THIS A SUBSTANTIAL MAIN COURSE SOUP. BASMATI OR THAI RICE HAS THE BEST FLAVOUR, BUT ANY LONG GRAIN RICE COULD BE USED. IF USING A QUICK-COOK RICE, COOK THE VEGETABLES FOR LONGER BEFORE ADDING THE RICE.

SERVES FOUR TO SIX

INGREDIENTS

450g/1lb fresh mussels
about 250ml/8fl oz/1 cup white wine
675–900g/1½–2lb mixed white fish
  fillets such as monkfish, plaice,
  flounder, cod or haddock
6 large scallops
30ml/2 tbsp olive oil
3 leeks, chopped
1 garlic clove, crushed
1 red (bell) pepper, seeded and cut
  into 2.5cm/1in pieces
1 yellow (bell) pepper, seeded and
  cut into 2.5cm/1in pieces
175g/6oz fennel, cut into
  4cm/1½in pieces
400g/14oz can chopped tomatoes
about 1.2 litres/2 pints/5 cups
  well-flavoured fish stock
generous pinch of saffron threads,
  soaked in 15ml/1 tbsp hot water
175g/6oz/scant 1 cup basmati
  rice, soaked
8 large raw prawns (shrimp), peeled
  and deveined
salt and ground black pepper
30–45ml/2–3 tbsp fresh dill,
  to garnish
crusty bread, to serve (optional)

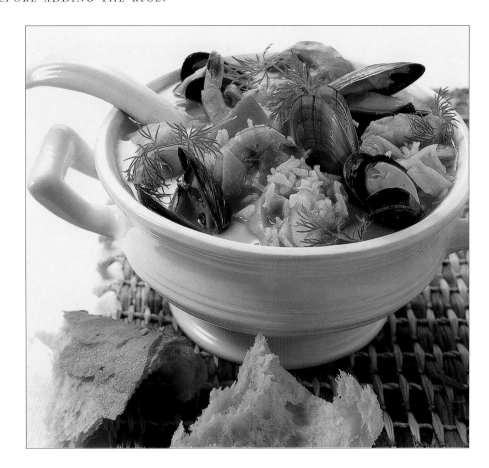

1 Scrub the mussels and pull off the beards, discarding any shellfish that do not close when tapped with a knife. Place them in a heavy pan. Add 90ml/ 6 tbsp of the wine, cover tightly, bring to the boil over a high heat and cook, shaking the pan occasionally, for about 3 minutes or until all the mussels have opened. Strain, reserving the liquid. Set aside half the mussels in their shells for the garnish; shell the rest and put them in a bowl. Discard any mussels that have not opened.

2 Cut the fish into 2.5cm/1in cubes. Detach the corals from the scallops and slice the white flesh into three or four pieces. Add the scallops to the fish and the corals to the mussels.

3 Heat the olive oil in a pan and cook the leeks and garlic for 3–4 minutes, until softened. Add the peppers and fennel and cook for 2 minutes more.

4 Add the tomatoes, stock, saffron water, reserved mussel liquid and the remaining wine. Season well and cook for 5 minutes. Drain the rice, stir it into the mixture, cover and simmer for 10 minutes, until it is just tender.

5 Carefully stir in the white fish and cook over a low heat for 5 minutes. Add the prawns and cook for a further 2 minutes, then add the scallop corals and mussels and cook for 2–3 minutes more, until all the fish is tender. If the soup seems dry, add a little extra white wine or stock, or a little of both. Spoon into warmed soup dishes, top with the mussels in their shells and sprinkle with the dill. Serve with fresh crusty bread, if you like.

COOK'S TIP
To make your own fish stock, place about 450g/1lb white fish trimmings – bones, heads, but not gills – in a large pan. Add a chopped onion, carrot, bay leaf, fresh parsley sprig, 6 peppercorns and a 5cm/ 2in piece of pared lemon rind. Pour in 1.2 litres/2 pints/5 cups water, bring to the boil and simmer for 25–30 minutes. Strain through muslin (cheesecloth).

Per portion: Energy 544Kcal/2283kJ; Protein 55.9g; Carbohydrate 49.2g, of which sugars 11.7g; Fat 9.3g, of which saturates 1.4g; Cholesterol 143mg; Calcium 177mg; Fibre 5.6g; Sodium 325mg.

CLAM CHOWDER

IF FRESH CLAMS ARE HARD TO FIND, USE FROZEN OR CANNED CLAMS FOR THIS CLASSIC RECIPE FROM NEW ENGLAND. LARGE CLAMS SHOULD BE CUT INTO CHUNKY PIECES. RESERVE A FEW CLAMS IN THEIR SHELLS FOR GARNISH, IF YOU LIKE. TRADITIONALLY, THE SOUP IS SERVED WITH SAVOURY BISCUITS CALLED SALTINE CRACKERS. YOU SHOULD BE ABLE TO FIND THESE IN ANY GOOD DELICATESSEN.

SERVES FOUR

INGREDIENTS
    100g/3¾oz salt pork or thinly sliced
        unsmoked bacon, diced
    1 large onion, chopped
    2 potatoes, peeled and cut into
        1cm/½in cubes
    1 bay leaf
    1 fresh thyme sprig
    300ml/½ pint/1¼ cups milk
    400g/14oz cooked clams, cooking
        liquid reserved
    150ml/¼ pint/⅔ cup double
        (heavy) cream
    salt, ground white pepper and
        cayenne pepper
    finely chopped fresh parsley, to garnish

1 Put the salt pork or unsmoked bacon in a pan, and heat gently, stirring frequently, until the fat runs and the meat is starting to brown. Add the chopped onion and cook over a low heat, stirring occasionally, until softened but not browned.

2 Add the cubed potatoes, the bay leaf and thyme sprig, stir well to coat with fat, then pour in the milk and reserved clam liquid and bring to the boil. Lower the heat and simmer for about 10 minutes, until the potatoes are tender but still firm. Lift out the bay leaf and thyme sprig and discard.

3 Remove the shells from most of the clams. Add all the clams to the pan and season to taste with salt, pepper and cayenne. Simmer gently for 5 minutes more, then stir in the cream. Heat until the soup is very hot, but do not allow it to boil. Pour into a warmed tureen, garnish with the chopped fresh parsley and serve immediately.

CHINESE CRAB AND CORN SOUP

FROZEN WHITE CRAB MEAT WORKS AS WELL AS FRESH IN THIS DELICATELY FLAVOURED SOUP.

SERVES FOUR

INGREDIENTS
    600ml/1 pint/2½ cups fish or
        chicken stock
    2.5cm/1in fresh root ginger, very
        thinly sliced
    400g/14oz can creamed corn
    150g/5oz cooked white crab meat
    15ml/1 tbsp arrowroot or
        cornflour (cornstarch)
    15ml/1 tbsp Chinese rice wine or
        dry sherry
    15–30ml/1–2 tbsp light soy sauce
    1 egg white
    salt and ground white pepper
    shredded spring onions (scallions),
        to garnish

COOK'S TIP
This soup is sometimes made with whole kernel corn, but creamed corn gives a better texture. If you can't find it in a can, use thawed frozen creamed corn instead; the result will be just as good.

1 Put the stock and ginger in a large, heavy pan and bring to the boil over a medium heat. Stir in the creamed corn and bring back to the boil.

2 Turn off the heat and add the crab meat. Put the arrowroot or cornflour in a cup and stir in the rice wine or sherry to make a smooth paste, then stir this into the soup. Cook over a low heat for about 3 minutes, until the soup has thickened and is slightly glutinous in consistency. Add light soy sauce, salt and white pepper to taste.

3 In a bowl, whisk the egg white to a stiff foam. Gradually fold it into the soup. Ladle the soup into heated bowls, garnish each portion with spring onions and serve immediately.

VARIATION
To make prawn (shrimp) and corn soup, substitute 150g/5oz cooked peeled and deveined prawns for the crab meat. Chop the peeled prawns coarsely and add to the soup at the beginning of step 2.

Top per portion: Energy 439Kcal/1829kJ; Protein 25.6g; Carbohydrate 25.9g, of which sugars 8.8g; Fat 26.6g, of which saturates 15.2g; Cholesterol 136mg; Calcium 204mg; Fibre 1.8g; Sodium 1638mg.
Below per portion: Energy 201Kcal/852kJ; Protein 11.3g; Carbohydrate 33.8g, of which sugars 9.9g; Fat 3.2g, of which saturates 0.5g; Cholesterol 27mg; Calcium 17mg; Fibre 1.4g; Sodium 695mg.

SEAFOOD LAKSA

A LAKSA IS A CHUNKY MALAYSIAN SOUP OF FISH, POULTRY, MEAT OR VEGETABLES WITH NOODLES.
AUTHENTIC LAKSAS ARE OFTEN HOT, AND COOLED BY THE COCONUT MILK AND THE NOODLES. IF YOU
WOULD PREFER A HOTTER VERSION, ADD A LITTLE CHILLI POWDER INSTEAD OF SOME OF THE PAPRIKA.

SERVES FOUR TO FIVE

INGREDIENTS

   3 medium-hot fresh red
     chillies, seeded
   4–5 garlic cloves
   5ml/1 tsp mild paprika
   10ml/2 tsp fermented shrimp paste
   25ml/1½ tbsp chopped fresh root
     ginger or galangal
   250g/9oz small red shallots
   25g/1oz fresh coriander (cilantro),
     preferably with roots
   45ml/3 tbsp groundnut (peanut) oil
   5ml/1 tsp fennel seeds, crushed
   2 fennel bulbs, cut into thin wedges
   600ml/1 pint/2½ cups fish stock
   300g/11oz thin vermicelli
     rice noodles
   450ml/¾ pint/scant 2 cups
     coconut milk
   juice of 1–2 limes
   30–45ml/2–3 tbsp Thai fish sauce
   450g/1lb firm white fish fillet, such
     as monkfish, halibut or snapper
   450g/1lb large raw prawns (shrimp)
     (about 20), peeled and deveined
   small bunch of fresh holy basil or
     ordinary basil
   2 spring onions (scallions),
     thinly sliced

1 Put the chillies, garlic, paprika, shrimp paste, ginger or galangal and 2 shallots in a food processor, blender or spice grinder and process to a paste. Remove the roots and stems from the coriander and add them to the paste; chop and reserve the coriander leaves. Add 15ml/1 tbsp of the oil to the paste and process again until fairly smooth.

2 Heat the remaining oil in a large pan. Add the remaining shallots, the fennel seeds and fennel wedges. Cook over a medium heat, stirring occasionally, until lightly browned, then add 45ml/3 tbsp of the spice paste and stir-fry for about 1–2 minutes. Pour in the fish stock and bring to the boil. Reduce the heat and simmer for 8–10 minutes.

3 Meanwhile, cook the vermicelli rice noodles according to the packet instructions. Drain and set aside.

4 Add the coconut milk and the juice of 1 lime to the pan of shallots. Stir in 30ml/2 tbsp of the fish sauce. Bring to a simmer and taste, adding a little more spice paste, lime juice or fish sauce as necessary.

5 Cut the fish into chunks and add to the pan. Cook for 2–3 minutes, then add the prawns and cook until they turn pink. Chop most of the basil and add to the pan with the reserved coriander.

6 Divide the noodles among wide bowls, then ladle in the soup. Sprinkle with spring onions and the remaining whole basil leaves. Serve immediately.

Per portion: Energy 524Kcal/2199kJ; Protein 43.1g; Carbohydrate 65.1g, of which sugars 6.3g; Fat 10.1g, of which saturates 2g; Cholesterol 233mg; Calcium 162mg; Fibre 1.9g; Sodium 356mg.

BOUILLABAISSE

AUTHENTIC BOUILLABAISSE COMES FROM THE SOUTH OF FRANCE AND INCLUDES RASCASSE (SCORPION FISH) AS AN ESSENTIAL INGREDIENT. IT IS, HOWEVER, PERFECTLY POSSIBLE TO MAKE THIS WONDERFUL MAIN-COURSE SOUP WITHOUT IT. USE AS LARGE A VARIETY OF FISH AS YOU CAN.

SERVES FOUR

INGREDIENTS

    45ml/3 tbsp olive oil
    2 onions, chopped
    2 leeks, white parts only, chopped
    4 garlic cloves, chopped
    450g/1lb ripe tomatoes, peeled
      and chopped
    3 litres/5 pints/12 cups boiling fish
      stock or water
    15ml/1 tbsp tomato purée (paste)
    large pinch of saffron threads
    1 fresh bouquet garni, containing
      2 thyme sprigs, 2 bay leaves and
      2 fennel sprigs
    3kg/6½lb mixed fish, cleaned and
      cut into large chunks
    4 potatoes, peeled and
      thickly sliced
    salt, pepper and cayenne pepper
    a bowl of Rouille and a bowl of
      Aioli, to serve
For the garnish
    16 slices of French bread, toasted
      and rubbed with garlic
    30ml/2 tbsp chopped fresh parsley

2 Simmer the soup for 5–8 minutes, removing each type of fish as it becomes cooked. Continue to cook until the potatoes are very tender. Season well with salt, pepper and cayenne.

3 Divide the fish and potatoes among individual soup plates. Strain the soup and ladle it over the fish. Garnish with toasted French bread and parsley. Serve with rouille and aioli.

1 Heat the oil in a large pan. Add the onions, leeks, garlic and tomatoes. Cook until slightly softened. Stir in the stock or water, tomato purée and saffron. Add the bouquet garni and boil until the oil is amalgamated. Lower the heat; add the fish and potatoes.

COOK'S TIP
Suitable fish for Bouillabaisse include rascasse, conger eel, monkfish, red gurnard and John Dory.

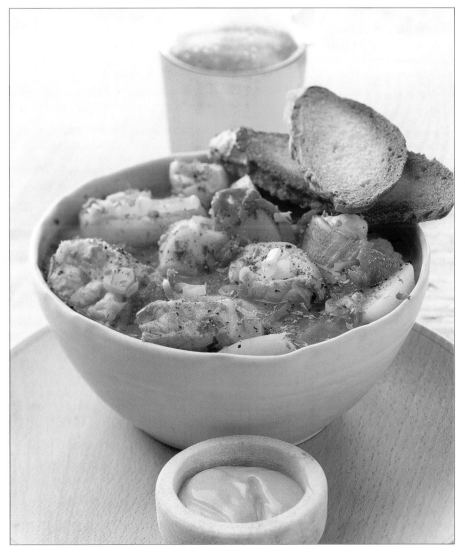

Per portion: Energy 814Kcal/3426kJ; Protein 142.3g; Carbohydrate 28.1g, of which sugars 10.8g; Fat 15.1g, of which saturates 2.2g; Cholesterol 345mg; Calcium 121mg; Fibre 4.9g; Sodium 895mg.

MEDITERRANEAN LEEK AND FISH SOUP WITH TOMATOES

THIS CHUNKY SOUP, WHICH IS ALMOST A STEW, MAKES A ROBUST AND WONDERFULLY AROMATIC MEAL IN A BOWL. SERVE IT WITH CRISP-BAKED CROÛTES SPREAD WITH A SPICY GARLIC MAYONNAISE.

SERVES FOUR

INGREDIENTS
30ml/2 tbsp olive oil
2 large thick leeks, white and green
  parts separated, both thinly sliced
5ml/1 tsp crushed coriander seeds
good pinch of dried red chilli flakes
300g/11oz salad potatoes, sliced
200g/7oz can Italian peeled
  chopped plum tomatoes
600ml/1 pint/2½ cups fish stock
150ml/¼ pint/⅔ cup fruity white wine
1 fresh bay leaf
1 star anise
strip of pared orange rind
good pinch of saffron threads
450g/1lb white fish fillets, such as
  monkfish, sea bass, cod or haddock
450g/1lb small squid, cleaned
250g/9oz uncooked peeled
  prawns (shrimp)
30–45ml/2–3 tbsp chopped parsley
salt and ground black pepper
To serve
1 short French loaf, sliced and toasted
spicy garlic mayonnaise

1 Gently heat the oil in a pan, then add the green part of the leeks, the coriander and chilli and cook for 5 minutes.

2 Add the potatoes and tomatoes and pour in the stock and wine. Add the bay leaf, star anise, orange rind and saffron.

3 Bring to the boil, reduce the heat and part-cover the pan. Simmer for 20 minutes, or until the potatoes are tender. Taste and adjust the seasoning.

4 Cut the fish into chunks. Cut the squid sacs into rectangles and score a criss-cross pattern into them without cutting right through.

5 Add the fish to the soup and cook gently for 4 minutes. Add the prawns and cook for 1 minute. Add the squid and the shredded white part of the leek and cook, stirring occasionally, for 2 minutes.

6 Stir in the chopped parsley and serve with toasted French bread and spicy garlic mayonnaise.

Per portion: Energy 326Kcal/1379kJ; Protein 49.7g; Carbohydrate 17.5g, of which sugars 4.4g; Fat 4.2g, of which saturates 0.9g; Cholesterol 421mg; Calcium 106mg; Fibre 2.9g; Sodium 333mg.

FISH SOUP <u>WITH</u> ROUILLE

MAKING THIS SOUP IS SIMPLICITY ITSELF, ALTHOUGH THE EXQUISITE FLAVOUR SUGGESTS IT IS THE PRODUCT OF PAINSTAKING PREPARATION AND COOKING.

SERVES SIX

INGREDIENTS
  1kg/2¼lb mixed fish
  30ml/2 tbsp olive oil
  1 onion, chopped
  1 carrot, chopped
  1 leek, chopped
  2 large ripe tomatoes, chopped
  1 red (bell) pepper, seeded
    and chopped
  2 garlic cloves, peeled
  150g/5oz/⅔ cup tomato
    purée (paste)
  1 large fresh bouquet garni,
    containing 3 parsley sprigs, 3 celery
    sticks and 3 bay leaves
  300ml/½ pint/1¼ cups white wine
  salt and ground black pepper
For the rouille
  2 garlic cloves, coarsely chopped
  5ml/1 tsp coarse salt
  1 thick slice of white bread, crust
    removed, soaked in water and
    squeezed dry
  1 fresh red chilli, seeded and
    coarsely chopped
  45ml/3 tbsp olive oil
  salt and cayenne pepper
For the garnish
  12 slices of baguette, toasted in
    the oven
  50g/2oz/½ cup grated Gruyère cheese

1 Cut the fish into 7.5cm/3in chunks, removing any obvious bones. Heat the oil in a large, heavy pan, then add the fish, onion, carrot, leek, tomatoes and red pepper. Cook over a medium heat, stirring occasionally, until the vegetables begin to colour.

2 Add all the other soup ingredients, then pour in just enough cold water to cover the mixture. Season well and bring to just below boiling point, then lower the heat to a bare simmer, cover and cook for 1 hour.

3 Meanwhile, make the rouille. Put the garlic and coarse salt in a mortar and crush to a paste with a pestle. Add the soaked bread and chilli and pound until smooth, or purée in a food processor. Whisk in the olive oil, a drop at a time, to make a smooth, shiny sauce that resembles mayonnaise. Season with salt and add a pinch of cayenne if you like a fiery taste. Set the rouille aside.

4 Lift out and discard the bouquet garni from the soup. Purée the soup in batches in a food processor, then strain through a fine sieve placed over a clean pan, pushing the solids through with the back of a ladle.

5 Reheat the soup without letting it boil. Check the seasoning and ladle into individual bowls. Top each serving with two slices of toasted baguette, a spoonful of rouille and some grated Gruyère.

COOK'S TIP
Any firm fish can be used for this recipe. If you use whole fish, include the heads, which enhance the flavour of the soup.

Per portion: Energy 513Kcal/2159kJ; Protein 41.3g; Carbohydrate 48.2g, of which sugars 11.7g; Fat 14.8g, of which saturates 3.6g; Cholesterol 85mg; Calcium 192mg; Fibre 4.4g; Sodium 642mg.

MISO SOUP WITH PORK AND VEGETABLES

THIS IS QUITE A RICH AND FILLING SOUP. ITS JAPANESE NAME, TANUKI JIRU, MEANS RACCOON SOUP FOR HUNTERS, BUT AS RACCOONS ARE NOT EATEN NOWADAYS, PORK IS NOW USED.

SERVES FOUR

INGREDIENTS
    200g/7oz lean boneless pork
    15cm/6in piece gobo or 1 parsnip
    50g/2oz mooli (daikon)
    4 fresh shiitake mushrooms
    ½ konnyaku or ½ × 225–285g/
        8–10¼oz packet tofu
    a little sesame oil, for stir-frying
    600ml/1 pint/2½ cups dashi stock, or
        the same amount of water and
        10ml/2 tsp dashi-no-moto
    70ml/4½ tbsp miso
    2 spring onions (scallions), chopped
    5ml/1 tsp sesame seeds

1 Press the meat down on a chopping board using the palm of your hand and slice horizontally into very thin long strips, then cut the strips crossways into small pieces. Set the pork aside.

2 Peel the gobo using a potato peeler, then cut diagonally into 1cm/½in thick slices. Quickly plunge the slices into a bowl of cold water to stop them discolouring. If you are using parsnip, peel, cut it in half lengthways, then cut it into 1cm/½in thick half-moon-shaped slices.

3 Peel and slice the mooli into 1.5cm/⅔in thick discs. Cut the discs into 1.5cm/⅔in cubes. Remove the shiitake stalks and cut the caps into quarters.

4 Place the konnyaku in a pan of boiling water and cook for 1 minute. Drain and cool. Cut in quarters lengthways, then crossways into 3mm/⅛in thick pieces.

5 Heat a little sesame oil in a heavy cast-iron or enamelled pan until purple smoke rises. Stir-fry the pork, then add the tofu, if using, the konnyaku and all the vegetables except for the spring onions. When the colour of the meat has changed, add the stock.

6 Bring to the boil over a medium heat, and skim off the foam until the soup looks fairly clear. Reduce the heat, cover, and simmer for 15 minutes.

7 Put the miso in a small bowl, and mix with 60ml/4 tbsp hot stock to make a smooth paste. Stir one-third of the miso into the soup. Taste and add a little more miso if required. Add the spring onion and remove from the heat. Serve very hot in individual soup bowls and sprinkle with sesame seeds.

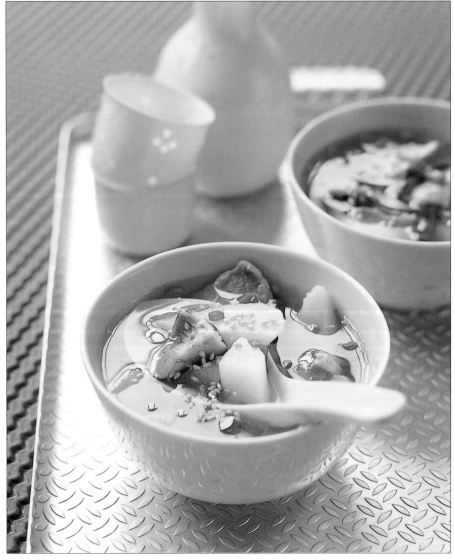

Per portion: Energy 114Kcal/475kJ; Protein 15.8g; Carbohydrate 1g, of which sugars 0.8g; Fat 5.2g, of which saturates 1.1g; Cholesterol 32mg; Calcium 306mg; Fibre 0.4g; Sodium 41mg.

CHUNKY LAMB AND CHICKPEA BROTH

*THIS JEWISH DISH OF SAVOURY MEATS AND BEANS IS BAKED IN A VERY LOW OVEN FOR SEVERAL HOURS.
A PARCEL OF RICE IS OFTEN ADDED TO THE BROTH PART-WAY THROUGH COOKING, WHICH PRODUCES A
LIGHTLY PRESSED RICE WITH A SLIGHTLY CHEWY TEXTURE.*

SERVES EIGHT

INGREDIENTS
   250g/9oz/1 cup chickpeas,
      soaked overnight
   45ml/3 tbsp olive oil
   1 onion, chopped
   10 garlic cloves, chopped
   1 parsnip, sliced
   3 carrots, sliced
   5–10ml/1–2 tsp ground cumin
   2.5ml/½ tsp ground turmeric
   15ml/1 tbsp chopped fresh root ginger
   2 litres/3½ pints/8 cups beef stock
   1 potato, peeled and cut into chunks
   ½ marrow (large zucchini), sliced or
      cut into chunks
   400g/14oz fresh or canned
      tomatoes, diced
   45–60ml/3–4 tbsp brown or
      green lentils
   2 bay leaves
   250g/9oz salted meat such as salt
      beef or corned beef (or double the
      quantity of lamb)
   250g/9oz piece of lamb
   ½ large bunch fresh coriander
      (cilantro), chopped
   200g/7oz/1 cup long grain rice
   1 lemon, cut into wedges and a spicy
      sauce or fresh chillies, finely
      chopped, to serve

1 Preheat the oven to 120°C/250°F/
Gas ½. Drain the chickpeas.

2 Heat the oil in a large flameproof
casserole, add the onion, garlic,
parsnip, carrots, cumin, turmeric and
ginger and cook for 2–3 minutes. Add
the chickpeas, stock, potato, marrow,
tomatoes, lentils, bay leaves, salted
meat, lamb and coriander. Cover and
cook in the oven for about 3 hours.

COOK'S TIP
Add 1–2 pinches of bicarbonate of soda
(baking soda) to the soaking chickpeas
to make them tender, but do not add too
much as it can make them mushy.

3 Put the rice on a double thickness of
muslin (cheesecloth) and tie together
at the corners, leaving enough room for
the rice to expand while it is cooking.

4 Two hours before the end of cooking,
remove the casserole from the oven.
Place the rice parcel in the casserole,
anchoring the edge of the muslin parcel
under the lid so that the parcel is held
above the soup and allowed to steam.
Return the casserole to the oven and
continue cooking for a further 2 hours.

5 Carefully remove the lid and the rice.
Skim any fat off the top of the soup
and ladle the soup into warm bowls with
a scoop of the rice and one or two
pieces of meat. Serve with lemon
wedges and a spoonful of hot sauce or
chopped fresh chillies.

Per portion: Energy 384Kcal/1619kJ; Protein 22.1g; Carbohydrate 46.8g, of which sugars 5.6g; Fat 13.4g, of which saturates 3.9g; Cholesterol 43mg; Calcium 95mg; Fibre 5.4g; Sodium 88mg.

Fragrant Beetroot and Vegetable Soup with Spiced Lamb Kubbeh

The Jewish community from Cochin in India is scattered now but they are still famous for their cuisine. This tangy soup is served with dumplings made of bright yellow pasta wrapped around a spicy lamb filling and a spoonful of fragrant green herb paste.

SERVES SIX TO EIGHT

INGREDIENTS
    15ml/1 tbsp vegetable oil
    ½ onion, finely chopped
    6 garlic cloves
    1 carrot, diced
    1 courgette (zucchini), diced
    ½ celery stick, diced (optional)
    4–5 cardamom pods
    2.5ml/½ tsp curry powder
    4 vacuum-packed beetroot (beets)
      (cooked not pickled), finely diced
      and juice reserved
    1 litre/1¾ pints/4 cups
      vegetable stock
    400g/14oz can chopped tomatoes
    45–60ml/3–4 tbsp chopped fresh
      coriander (cilantro) leaves
    2 bay leaves
    15ml/1 tbsp sugar
    salt and ground black pepper
    15–30ml/1–2 tbsp white wine
      vinegar, to serve
For the kubbeh
    2 large pinches of saffron threads
    15ml/1 tbsp hot water
    15ml/1 tbsp vegetable oil
    1 large onion, chopped
    250g/9oz lean minced (ground) lamb
    5ml/1 tsp vinegar
    ½ bunch fresh mint, chopped
    115g/4oz/1 cup plain (all-purpose) flour
    2–3 pinches of salt
    2.5–5ml/½–1 tsp ground turmeric
    45–60ml/3–4 tbsp cold water
For the ginger and coriander paste
    4 garlic cloves, chopped
    15–25ml/1–1½ tbsp chopped
      fresh root ginger
    ½–4 fresh mild chillies
    ½ large bunch of fresh
      coriander (cilantro)
    30ml/2 tbsp white wine vinegar
    extra virgin olive oil

COOK'S TIP
Serve any leftover paste with meatballs or spread on sandwiches.

1 To make the paste, put the garlic, ginger and chillies in a food processor and process. Add the coriander, vinegar, oil and salt and process to a purée. Set aside.

2 To make the kubbeh filling, place the saffron and hot water in a small bowl and leave to infuse (steep). Meanwhile, heat the oil in a pan and cook the onion until softened. Put the onion and saffron water in a food processor and blend. Add the lamb, season and blend. Add the vinegar and mint, then chill.

3 To make the kubbeh dough, put the flour, salt and ground turmeric in a food processor, then gradually add the water, processing until it forms a sticky dough. Knead on a floured surface for 5 minutes, wrap in a plastic bag and leave to stand for 30 minutes.

4 Divide the dough into 10–15 pieces. Roll each into a ball, then, using a pasta machine, roll into very thin rounds.

5 Lay the rounds on a well-floured surface. Place a spoonful of filling in the middle of each. Dampen the edges of the dough, then bring them together and seal. Set aside on a floured surface.

6 To make the soup, heat the oil in a pan, add the onion and cook for about 10 minutes, or until softened but not browned. Add half the garlic, the carrot, courgette, celery, if using, cardamom pods and curry powder and cook for 2–3 minutes.

7 Add three of the diced beetroot, the stock, tomatoes, coriander, bay leaves and sugar to the pan. Bring to the boil, then reduce the heat and simmer for about 20 minutes.

8 Add the remaining beetroot, beetroot juice and garlic to the soup. Season with salt and pepper to taste and set aside until ready to serve.

9 To serve, reheat the soup and poach the dumplings in a large pan of salted boiling water for about 4 minutes. Using a slotted spoon, remove the dumplings from the water as they are cooked and place on a plate to keep warm.

10 Ladle the soup into bowls, adding a dash of vinegar to each bowl, then add two or three dumplings and a small spoonful of the ginger and coriander paste to each. Serve immediately.

Per portion: Energy 253Kcal/1061kJ; Protein 12.2g; Carbohydrate 26.6g, of which sugars 10.8g; Fat 11.6g, of which saturates 3.4g; Cholesterol 32mg; Calcium 73mg; Fibre 2.8g; Sodium 90mg.

THAI PRAWN SALAD WITH GARLIC DRESSING AND FRIZZLED SHALLOTS

IN THIS INTENSELY FLAVOURED SALAD, PRAWNS AND MANGO ARE PARTNERED WITH A SWEET-SOUR GARLIC DRESSING HEIGHTENED WITH THE HOT TASTE OF CHILLI. THE CRISP FRIZZLED SHALLOTS ARE A TRADITIONAL ADDITION TO THAI SALADS.

SERVES FOUR TO SIX

INGREDIENTS

675g/1½lb raw prawns (shrimp), peeled and deveined with tails on
finely shredded rind of 1 lime
½ fresh red chilli, seeded and finely chopped
30ml/2 tbsp olive oil, plus extra for brushing
1 ripe but firm mango
2 carrots, cut into long thin shreds
10cm/4in piece cucumber, sliced
1 small red onion, halved and thinly sliced
a few fresh coriander (cilantro) sprigs
a few fresh mint sprigs
45ml/3 tbsp roasted peanuts, coarsely chopped
4 large shallots, thinly sliced and fried until crisp in 30ml/2 tbsp groundnut (peanut) oil
salt and ground black pepper
For the dressing
1 large garlic clove, chopped
10–15ml/2–3 tsp caster (superfine) sugar
juice of 2 limes
15–30ml/1–2 tbsp Thai fish sauce
1 fresh red chilli, seeded
5–10ml/1–2 tsp light rice vinegar

1 Place the prawns in a glass or china dish and add the lime rind and chilli. Season with salt and pepper and spoon the oil over them. Toss to mix and leave to marinate for 30–40 minutes.

2 For the dressing, place the garlic in a mortar with 10ml/2 tsp caster sugar and pound until smooth, then work in the juice of 1½ limes and 15ml/1 tbsp of the Thai fish sauce.

3 Transfer the dressing to a jug (pitcher). Finely chop half the chilli. and add it to the dressing. Taste and add more sugar, lime juice, fish sauce and the rice vinegar to taste.

COOK'S TIP
To devein prawns, make a shallow cut down the back of the prawn using a small, sharp knife. Using the tip of the knife, lift out the thin, black vein, then rinse the prawn thoroughly under cold, running water.

4 Peel and stone (pit) the mango, then cut it into very fine strips.

5 Toss together the mango, carrots, cucumber and onion, and half the dressing. Arrange the salad on individual plates or in bowls.

6 Heat a ridged, cast-iron griddle pan or heavy frying pan until very hot. Brush with a little olive oil, then sear the prawns for 2–3 minutes on each side, until they turn pink and are patched with brown on the outside. Arrange the prawns on the salads.

7 Sprinkle the remaining dressing over the salads and top with the sprigs of coriander and mint. Finely shred the remaining chilli and sprinkle it over the salads with the peanuts and crisp-fried shallots. Serve immediately.

Per portion: Energy 349Kcal/1458kJ; Protein 33.5g; Carbohydrate 15.4g, of which sugars 13.7g; Fat 17.4g, of which saturates 3g; Cholesterol 329mg; Calcium 162mg; Fibre 2.8g; Sodium 596mg.

WHITEFISH SALAD

SMOKED WHITEFISH IS ONE OF THE GLORIES OF DELI FOOD AND, MADE INTO A SALAD WITH MAYONNAISE AND SOUR CREAM, IT BECOMES INDISPENSABLE AS A BRUNCH DISH. EAT IT WITH A STACK OF BAGELS, PUMPERNICKEL OR RYE BREAD. IF YOU CAN'T FIND SMOKED WHITEFISH, USE ANY OTHER SMOKED FIRM WHITE FISH, SUCH AS HALIBUT OR COD.

SERVES FOUR TO SIX

INGREDIENTS

1 smoked whitefish, skinned
  and boned
2 celery sticks, chopped
½ red, white or yellow onion
  or 3–5 spring onions
  (scallions), chopped
45ml/3 tbsp mayonnaise
45ml/3 tbsp sour cream or Greek
  (US strained plain) yogurt
juice of ½–1 lemon
1 round lettuce
ground black pepper
5–10ml/1–2 tsp chopped fresh
  parsley, to garnish

1 Break the smoked fish into bitesize pieces. In a bowl, combine the chopped celery, onion or spring onion, mayonnaise, and sour cream or yogurt, and add lemon juice to taste.

2 Fold the fish into the mixture and season with pepper. Arrange the lettuce leaves on serving plates, then spoon the whitefish salad on top. Serve chilled, sprinkled with parsley.

Per portion: Energy 172Kcal/719kJ; Protein 16g; Carbohydrate 4.3g, of which sugars 3.4g; Fat 10.4g, of which saturates 2g; Cholesterol 35mg; Calcium 62mg; Fibre 1.1g; Sodium 640mg.

WARM SALAD OF BAYONNE HAM AND NEW POTATOES

WITH A LIGHTLY SPICED NUTTY DRESSING, THIS WARM SALAD IS AS DELICIOUS AS IT IS FASHIONABLE, AND AN EXCELLENT CHOICE FOR INFORMAL ENTERTAINING.

SERVES FOUR

INGREDIENTS
    225g/8oz new potatoes, halved
      if large
    50g/2oz green beans
    115g/4oz young spinach leaves
    2 spring onions (scallions), sliced
    4 eggs, hard-boiled and quartered
    50g/2oz Bayonne ham, cut
      into strips
    juice of ½ lemon
    salt and ground black pepper
For the dressing
    60ml/4 tbsp olive oil
    5ml/1 tsp ground turmeric
    5ml/1 tsp ground cumin
    50g/2oz/½ cup shelled hazelnuts

1 Cook the potatoes in salted, boiling water for 10–15 minutes, or until tender, then drain. Cook the beans in salted, boiling water for 2 minutes, then drain.

2 Toss the potatoes and beans with the spinach and spring onions in a bowl.

3 Arrange the hard-boiled egg quarters on the salad and sprinkle the strips of ham over the top. Sprinkle with the lemon juice and season with plenty of salt and pepper.

4 Heat the dressing ingredients in a large frying pan and continue to cook, stirring frequently, until the nuts turn golden. Pour the hot, nutty dressing over the salad and serve immediately.

VARIATION
Replace the potatoes with a 400g/14oz can mixed beans and pulses. Drain and rinse the beans and pulses, then drain again. Toss lightly with the green beans and spring onions.

Per portion: Energy 323Kcal/1341kJ; Protein 12.4g; Carbohydrate 10.9g, of which sugars 2.2g; Fat 25.8g, of which saturates 4.2g; Cholesterol 199mg; Calcium 105mg; Fibre 2.3g; Sodium 270mg.

PERUVIAN SALAD

THIS REALLY IS A SPECTACULAR-LOOKING SALAD. IN PERU, WHITE RICE WOULD BE USED, BUT BROWN RICE ADDS AN INTERESTING TEXTURE AND FLAVOUR. IT MAKES A DELICIOUS LIGHT MEAL ON ITS OWN OR CAN BE SERVED WITH WARM, CRUSTY BREAD.

SERVES FOUR

INGREDIENTS
    225g/8oz/2 cups cooked long grain
        white or brown rice
    15ml/1 tbsp chopped fresh parsley
    1 red (bell) pepper
    1 small onion, sliced
    olive oil, for sprinkling
    115g/4oz green beans, halved
    50g/2oz/½ cup baby corn
    4 quail's eggs, hard-boiled
    25–50g/1–2oz Spanish ham, cut into
        thin slices (optional)
    1 small avocado
    lemon juice, for sprinkling
    75g/3oz mixed salad leaves
    15ml/1 tbsp capers
    about 10 stuffed olives, halved
For the dressing
    1 garlic clove, crushed
    60ml/4 tbsp olive oil
    45ml/3 tbsp sunflower oil
    30ml/2 tbsp lemon juice
    45ml/3 tbsp natural (plain) yogurt
    2.5ml/½ tsp mustard
    2.5ml/½ tsp sugar
    salt and freshly ground black pepper

1 Make the dressing by placing all the ingredients in a bowl and whisking with a fork until smooth. Alternatively, shake the ingredients together in a jam jar.

2 Put the cooked rice into a large, glass salad bowl and spoon in about half the dressing. Add the chopped parsley, stir well to mix and set aside in a cool place.

3 Cut the pepper in half, remove the seeds and pith, then place the halves, cut side down, in a small roasting pan. Add the onion rings. Sprinkle the onion with a little olive oil, place the pan under a hot grill (broiler) and cook for 5–6 minutes, until the pepper blackens and blisters and the onion turns golden. You may need to stir the onion once or twice so that it grills (broils) evenly.

4 Stir the onion in with the rice. Put the pepper in a plastic bag and knot the bag. When the steam has loosened the skin on the pepper halves and they are cool enough to handle, peel them and cut the flesh into thin strips.

COOK'S TIP
This dish looks particularly attractive if served in a deep, glass salad bowl. Guests can then see the various layers, starting with the white rice, then the green salad leaves, topped by the bright colours of peppers, corn, eggs and olives.

5 Cook the green beans in boiling water for 2 minutes, then add the corn and cook for 1–2 minutes more, until tender. Drain both vegetables, refresh them under cold water, then drain again. Place in a large mixing bowl and add the red pepper strips, quails' eggs and ham, if using.

6 Peel the avocado, remove the stone (pit), and cut the flesh into slices or chunks. Sprinkle with the lemon juice to prevent discoloration. Put the salad leaves in a separate mixing bowl, add the avocado and mix lightly. Arrange the salad on top of the rice.

7 Stir about 45ml/3 tbsp of the remaining dressing into the green bean and pepper mixture. Pile this on top of the salad.

8 Sprinkle the capers and stuffed olives on top and serve the salad with the remaining dressing.

Per portion: Energy 404Kcal/1675kJ; Protein 6.3g; Carbohydrate 25.6g, of which sugars 6.9g; Fat 31.3g, of which saturates 5.2g; Cholesterol 58mg; Calcium 75mg; Fibre 3.7g; Sodium 598mg.

Chicken and Mango Salad with Orange Rice

This fresh and delicious recipe draws its inspiration from all over the world.

SERVES FOUR

INGREDIENTS
15ml/1 tbsp sunflower oil
1 onion, chopped
1 garlic clove, crushed
30ml/2 tbsp red curry paste
10ml/2 tsp apricot jam
30ml/2 tbsp chicken stock
about 450g/1lb cooked chicken, cut
  into small pieces
150ml/¼ pint/⅔ cup natural
  (plain) yogurt
60–75ml/4–5 tbsp mayonnaise
1 large mango, peeled, stoned
  (pitted) and cut into 1cm/½in dice
fresh flat leaf parsley sprigs,
  to garnish
poppadums, to serve
For the orange rice
175g/6oz/scant 1 cup white long
  grain rice
225g/8oz carrots, grated
  (about 1⅓ cups)
1 large orange, cut
  into segments
40g/1½oz/⅓ cup roasted flaked
  (sliced) almonds
For the dressing
45ml/3 tbsp olive oil
60ml/4 tbsp sunflower oil
45ml/3 tbsp lemon juice
1 garlic clove, crushed
15ml/1 tbsp chopped mixed fresh
  herbs, such as tarragon, parsley,
  chives
salt and freshly ground black pepper

1 Heat the oil in a frying pan. Add the onion and garlic and cook over a medium heat, stirring occasionally, for 3–4 minutes, until soft.

2 Stir in the curry paste and cook for about 1 minute, stirring constantly, then lower the heat and stir in the apricot jam and chicken stock. Mix well, then add the chopped chicken and stir until it is thoroughly coated in the paste. Spoon into a bowl, cover with clear film (plastic wrap) and leave to cool.

3 Meanwhile, boil the rice in plenty of lightly salted water until just tender. Drain, rinse under cold water and drain again. When cool, stir into the grated carrots and add the orange segments and flaked almonds.

4 Make the dressing by whisking all the ingredients together in a bowl.

5 When the chicken mixture is cool, stir in the yogurt and mayonnaise, then add the mango, stirring it in carefully so as not to break the flesh. Chill for about 30 minutes.

6 When ready to serve, pour the dressing into the rice salad and mix well. Spoon on to a platter and mound the cold curried chicken on top. Garnish with flat leaf parsley and serve with poppadums.

COOK'S TIP
A simple way of dicing a mango is to take two thick slices from either side of the large flat stone (pit) without peeling the fruit. Make criss-cross cuts in the flesh on each slice and then turn inside out. The cubes of flesh will stand proud of the skin and can be easily cut off.

Per portion: Energy 776Kcal/3245kJ; Protein 35.9g; Carbohydrate 60.2g, of which sugars 21.1g; Fat 45.3g, of which saturates 6.4g; Cholesterol 93mg; Calcium 172mg; Fibre 4.5g; Sodium 206mg.

THAI BEEF SALAD

ALL THE INGREDIENTS FOR THIS TRADITIONAL THAI DISH — KNOWN AS YAM NUA YANG *— ARE WIDELY AVAILABLE IN LARGER SUPERMARKETS.*

SERVES FOUR

INGREDIENTS
675g/1½lb fillet steak
(beef tenderloin)
30ml/2 tbsp olive oil
2 small mild red chillies, seeded
and sliced
225g/8oz/3¼ cups shiitake
mushrooms, sliced
For the dressing
3 spring onions (scallions), chopped
2 garlic cloves, finely chopped
juice of 1 lime
15–30ml/1–2 tbsp fish or oyster
sauce, to taste
5ml/1 tsp soft light brown sugar
30ml/2 tbsp chopped fresh
coriander (cilantro)
To serve
1 cos or romaine lettuce, torn
into strips
175g/6oz cherry tomatoes, halved
5cm/2in piece cucumber, peeled,
halved and thinly sliced
45ml/3 tbsp toasted sesame seeds

1 Preheat the grill (broiler), then cook the steak for 2–4 minutes on each side depending on how well done you like steak. Leave to cool for at least 15 minutes.

2 Use a very sharp knife to slice the meat as thinly as possible and place the slices in a bowl.

VARIATION
If you can find them, yellow chillies make a colourful addition to this dish. Substitute one for one of the red chillies.

3 Heat the olive oil in a small frying pan. Add the seeded and sliced red chillies and the sliced mushrooms and cook for 5 minutes, stirring occasionally. Turn off the heat and add the grilled (broiled) steak slices to the pan, then stir well to coat the slices in the chilli and mushroom mixture.

4 Stir all the ingredients for the dressing together, then pour it over the meat mixture and toss gently.

5 Arrange the salad ingredients on a serving plate. Spoon the warm steak mixture into the centre and sprinkle the sesame seeds over, then serve.

Per portion: Energy 381Kcal/1591kJ; Protein 39.8g; Carbohydrate 4.1g, of which sugars 3.8g; Fat 23g, of which saturates 6.6g; Cholesterol 103mg; Calcium 105mg; Fibre 2.5g; Sodium 352mg.

FISH

Pan-fried, roasted or baked, fish forms the basis of countless elegant recipes. Choose a rich, hearty dish such as Fillets of Brill in Red Wine Sauce, flavoursome Roast Monkfish with Garlic, or if you want something you can prepare in advance, try Smoked Fish and Asparagus Mousse, or an impressive whole Baked Salmon with Watercress Sauce.

  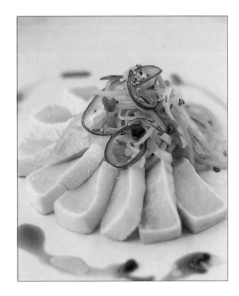

STRIPED FISH TERRINE

*SERVE THIS ATTRACTIVE TERRINE COLD OR JUST WARM, WITH A HOLLANDAISE SAUCE IF YOU LIKE.
IT IS IDEAL FOR A SUMMER LUNCHEON OR BUFFET.*

SERVES EIGHT

INGREDIENTS
15ml/1 tbsp sunflower oil
450g/1lb salmon fillet, skinned
450g/1lb sole fillets, skinned
3 egg whites
105ml/7 tbsp double (heavy) cream
15ml/1 tbsp finely chopped
  fresh chives
juice of 1 lemon
115g/4oz/1 cup fresh or frozen
  peas, cooked
5ml/1 tsp chopped fresh mint leaves
salt, ground white pepper and
  grated nutmeg
thinly sliced cucumber, salad cress
  and chives, to garnish

1 Grease a 1 litre/1¾ pint/4 cup loaf tin (pan) or terrine with the oil. Slice the salmon thinly, then cut it and the sole into long strips, 2.5cm/1in wide. Preheat the oven to 200°C/400°F/Gas 6.

2 Line the terrine neatly with alternate slices of salmon and sole, leaving the ends overhanging the edge. You should be left with about a third of the salmon and half the sole.

3 In a grease-free bowl, beat the egg whites with a pinch of salt until they form soft peaks. Purée the remaining sole in a food processor. Spoon into a mixing bowl, season, then fold in two-thirds of the egg whites, followed by two-thirds of the cream. Put half the mixture into a second bowl; stir in the chives. Add nutmeg to the first bowl.

4 Purée the remaining salmon, scrape it into a bowl; add the lemon juice. Fold in the remaining whites, then the cream.

5 Process the peas and mint. Season the mixture and spread it over the base of the terrine, smoothing the surface with a spatula. Spoon over the sole with chives mixture and spread evenly.

6 Add the salmon mixture, then finish with the plain sole mixture. Cover with the overhanging fish fillets and make a lid of oiled foil. Stand the terrine in a roasting pan and pour in enough boiling water to come halfway up the sides.

7 Bake for 15–20 minutes, until the top fillets are just cooked and the mousse feels springy. Remove the foil, lay a wire rack over the top of the terrine and invert both rack and terrine on to a lipped baking sheet to catch the cooking juices that drain out. Keep these to make fish stock or soup.

8 Leaving the tin in place, let the terrine stand for about 15 minutes, then turn the terrine over again. Invert it on to a serving dish and lift off the tin carefully. Serve warm, or chill in the refrigerator first and serve cold. Garnish with thinly sliced cucumber, salad cress and chives before serving.

COOK'S TIPS
• Put the salmon into the freezer about an hour before slicing it. If it is almost frozen, it will be much easier to slice.
• You can line the tin or terrine with oven-safe clear film (plastic wrap) after greasing and before adding the salmon and sole strips. This makes it a little easier to turn out the terrine but is not strictly necessary.

Per portion: Energy 245Kcal/1019kJ; Protein 23.8g; Carbohydrate 1.9g, of which sugars 0.6g; Fat 15.8g, of which saturates 5.7g; Cholesterol 74mg; Calcium 38mg; Fibre 0.7g; Sodium 107mg.

SALMON FISH CAKES

THE SECRET OF A GOOD FISH CAKE IS TO MAKE IT WITH FRESHLY PREPARED FISH AND POTATOES,
HOME-MADE BREADCRUMBS AND PLENTY OF INTERESTING SEASONING.

SERVES FOUR

INGREDIENTS
  450g/1lb cooked salmon fillet
  450g/1lb cooked potatoes, mashed
  25g/1oz/2 tbsp butter, melted
  10ml/2 tsp wholegrain mustard
  15ml/1 tbsp each chopped fresh dill
    and chopped fresh parsley
  grated rind and juice of ½ lemon
  15g/½oz/1 tbsp plain (all-
    purpose) flour
  1 egg, lightly beaten
  150g/5oz/1¼ cups dried breadcrumbs
  60ml/4 tbsp sunflower oil
  salt and ground black pepper
  rocket (arugula) leaves, chives and
    lemon wedges to garnish

1 Flake the cooked salmon, discarding any skin and bones. Put it in a bowl with the mashed potato, melted butter and wholegrain mustard and mix well. Stir in the dill and parsley and lemon rind and juice. Season to taste with salt and pepper.

2 Divide the mixture into eight portions and shape each into a ball, then flatten into a thick disc. Dip the fish cakes first in flour, then in egg and, finally, in breadcrumbs to coat evenly.

3 Heat the oil in a frying pan until it is very hot. Cook the fish cakes, in batches, until golden brown and crisp all over. As each batch is ready, drain on kitchen paper and keep hot. Garnish with rocket leaves and chives and serve with lemon wedges.

COOK'S TIP
Almost any fresh white or hot-smoked fish is suitable; smoked cod and haddock are particularly good.

Per portion: Energy 586Kcal/2453kJ; Protein 29.8g; Carbohydrate 49.9g, of which sugars 3.2g; Fat 31g, of which saturates 7.2g; Cholesterol 117mg; Calcium 79mg; Fibre 1.3g; Sodium 266mg.

SMOKED FISH <u>AND</u> ASPARAGUS MOUSSE

THIS ELEGANT MOUSSE LOOKS VERY SPECIAL WITH ITS STUDDING OF ASPARAGUS AND SMOKED SALMON.
SERVE A MUSTARD AND DILL DRESSING SEPARATELY IF YOU LIKE.

SERVES EIGHT

INGREDIENTS
   15ml/1 tbsp powdered gelatine
   juice of 1 lemon
   105ml/7 tbsp fish stock
   50g/2oz/¼ cup butter, plus extra
      for greasing
   2 shallots, finely chopped
   225g/8oz smoked trout fillets
   105ml/7 tbsp sour cream
   225g/8oz/1 cup low-fat cream cheese
      or cottage cheese
   1 egg white
   12 spinach leaves, blanched
   12 fresh asparagus spears,
      lightly cooked
   115g/4oz smoked salmon, cut into
      long strips
   salt
   shredded beetroot (beet) and leaves,
      to garnish

1 Sprinkle the gelatine over the lemon juice and leave until spongy. In a small pan, heat the fish stock, then add the soaked gelatine and stir to dissolve completely. Set aside. Melt the butter in a small pan, add the shallots and cook gently until softened but not coloured.

2 Break up the smoked trout fillets and put them in a food processor with the shallots, sour cream, stock mixture and cream or cottage cheese. Process until smooth, then spoon into a bowl.

3 In a clean bowl, beat the egg white with a pinch of salt to soft peaks. Fold into the fish. Cover the bowl and chill for 30 minutes, or until starting to set.

4 Grease a 1 litre/1¾ pint/4 cup loaf tin (pan) or terrine with butter, then line it with the spinach leaves. Carefully spread half the trout mousse over the spinach-covered base, arrange the asparagus spears on top, then cover with the remaining trout mousse.

5 Arrange the smoked salmon strips lengthways on the mousse and fold over the overhanging spinach leaves. Cover with clear film (plastic wrap) and chill for 4 hours, until set. To serve, remove the clear film, turn out on to a serving dish and garnish.

Per portion: Energy 174Kcal/723kJ; Protein 15.8g; Carbohydrate 2.8g, of which sugars 2.6g; Fat 11g, of which saturates 6g; Cholesterol 58mg; Calcium 75mg; Fibre 0.8g; Sodium 432mg.

SEARED SWORDFISH <u>WITH</u> CITRUS DRESSING

THIS CONTEMPORARY JAPANESE DISH TAKES CONVENTIONAL SALAD INGREDIENTS AND MIXES THEM WITH SHOYU, DASHI AND SESAME OIL FOR A BRIGHT, NEW TASTE. FRESH FISH IS SLICED THINLY AND SEARED OR MARINATED, THEN SERVED WITH SALAD LEAVES AND VEGETABLES.

SERVES FOUR

INGREDIENTS
    75g/3oz mooli (daikon), peeled
    50g/2oz carrot, peeled
    1 Japanese or salad cucumber
    10ml/2 tsp vegetable oil
    300g/11oz skinned fresh swordfish
      steak, cut against the grain
    2 cartons salad cress
    15ml/1 tbsp toasted
      sesame seeds
For the dressing
    105ml/7 tbsp shoyu
    105ml/7 tbsp second dashi stock,
      or the same amount of water and
      5ml/1 tsp dashi-no-moto
    30ml/2 tbsp toasted sesame oil
    juice of ½ lime
    rind of ½ lime, shredded into
      thin strips

1 Make the vegetable garnishes first. Use a very sharp knife, mandolin or vegetable slicer with a julienne blade to make very thin (about 4cm/1½in long) strands of mooli, carrot and cucumber. Soak the mooli and carrot in ice-cold water for 5 minutes, then drain well and keep in the refrigerator.

2 Mix together all the ingredients for the dressing and stir well, then chill.

3 Heat the oil in a small frying pan until smoking hot. Sear the fish for 30 seconds on all sides. Plunge it into cold water in a bowl to stop the cooking. Dry on kitchen paper and wipe off as much oil as possible.

4 Cut the swordfish steak in half lengthways before slicing it into 5mm/¼in thick pieces in the other direction, against the grain.

5 Arrange the fish slices in a ring on individual plates. Mix the vegetable strands, salad cress and sesame seeds. Fluff up with your hands, then shape them into a sphere. Gently place it in the centre of the plate, on the swordfish. Pour the dressing around the plate's edge and serve immediately.

COOK'S TIP
This dish is traditionally made with fillet cut with the grain. To prepare, cut it in half lengthways, then slice against the grain by holding a knife horizontally to the chopping board.

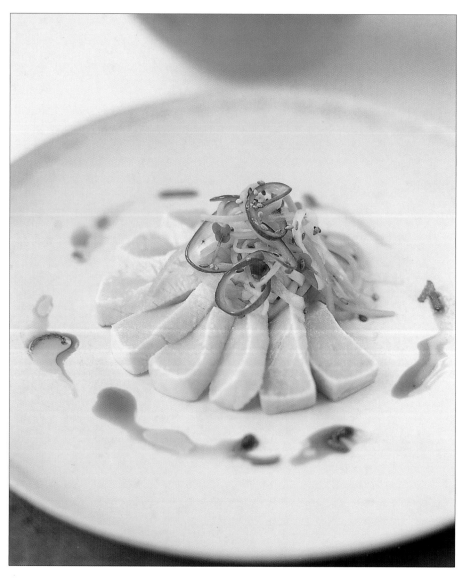

Per portion: Energy 192Kcal/799kJ; Protein 15.6g; Carbohydrate 4.1g, of which sugars 3.7g; Fat 12.7g, of which saturates 2g; Cholesterol 31mg; Calcium 53mg; Fibre 1.1g; Sodium 1887mg.

FILO-WRAPPED FISH

This delicious dish comes from Jerusalem, where whole fish are wrapped in filo pastry and served with a zesty tomato sauce. The choice of fish can be varied according to what is in season and what is freshest on the day of purchase.

SERVES THREE TO FOUR

INGREDIENTS

  450g/1lb salmon or cod steaks
    or fillets
  1 lemon
  30ml/2 tbsp olive oil, plus extra
    for brushing
  1 onion, chopped
  2 celery sticks, chopped
  1 green (bell) pepper, diced
  5 garlic cloves, chopped
  400g/14oz fresh or canned
    tomatoes, chopped
  120ml/4fl oz/½ cup passata
    (bottled strained tomatoes)
  30ml/2 tbsp chopped fresh flat
    leaf parsley
  2–3 pinches of ground allspice or
    ground cloves
  cayenne pepper, to taste
  pinch of sugar
  about 130g/4½oz filo pastry
    (6–8 large sheets)
  salt and ground black pepper

1 Sprinkle the salmon or cod steaks or fillets with salt and black pepper and a squeeze of lemon juice. Set aside while you prepare the sauce.

2 Heat the olive oil in a pan, add the chopped onion, celery and pepper and cook for about 5 minutes, until the vegetables are softened. Add the garlic and cook for a further 1 minute, then add the tomatoes and passata and cook until the tomatoes have softened and the mixture is of a sauce consistency.

3 Stir the parsley into the sauce, then season with allspice or cloves, cayenne pepper, sugar and salt and pepper.

4 Preheat the oven to 200°C/400°F/ Gas 6. Take a sheet of filo pastry, brush with a little olive oil and cover with a second sheet. Place a piece of fish on top of the pastry, towards the bottom edge, then top with 1–2 spoonfuls of the sauce, spreading it evenly.

5 Roll the fish in the pastry, taking care to enclose the filling completely. Arrange on a baking sheet and repeat with the remaining fish and pastry. You should have about half the sauce remaining, to serve with the fish.

6 Bake for 10–15 minutes, or until golden. Meanwhile, reheat the remaining sauce if necessary. Serve immediately with the remaining sauce.

Per portion: Energy 509Kcal/2135kJ; Protein 36.2g; Carbohydrate 37.2g, of which sugars 10.4g; Fat 25.1g, of which saturates 4.2g; Cholesterol 75mg; Calcium 137mg; Fibre 5g; Sodium 192mg.

STEAMED FISH WITH FIVE WILLOW SAUCE

A FISH KETTLE WILL COME IN USEFUL FOR THIS RECIPE. CARP IS TRADITIONALLY USED, BUT ANY CHUNKY FISH THAT CAN BE COOKED WHOLE, SUCH AS SALMON OR SEA BREAM, CAN BE GIVEN THIS TREATMENT. MAKE SURE YOU HAVE A SUITABLE LARGE PLATTER FOR SERVING THIS SPECTACULAR DISH.

SERVES FOUR

INGREDIENTS

1–2 carp or similar whole fish, total weight about 1kg/2¼ lb, cleaned and scaled

2.5cm/1in piece fresh root ginger, peeled and thinly sliced

4 spring onions (scallions), cut into thin strips

2.5ml/½ tsp salt

For the five willow sauce

375g/13oz jar chow chow (Chinese sweet mixed pickles)

300ml/½ pint/1¼ cups water

30ml/2 tbsp rice vinegar

25ml/1½ tbsp sugar

25ml/1½ tbsp cornflour (cornstarch)

15ml/1 tbsp light soy sauce

15ml/1 tbsp rice wine or medium-dry sherry

1 small green (bell) pepper, seeded and diced

1 carrot, peeled and cut into batons

1 tomato, peeled, seeded and diced

2 Fold up one or two pieces of foil to make a long wide strip. You will need one for each fish. Place the fish on the foil and then lift the fish on to the trivet. Lower the trivet into the fish kettle and tuck the ends of the foil over the fish.

3 Pour boiling water into the fish kettle to a depth of 2.5cm/1in. Bring to a full rolling boil, then lower the heat and cook the fish until the flesh flakes, topping up the kettle with boiling water as necessary. (See Cook's Tip for cooking times.)

5 In a small bowl, mix the cornflour to a paste with the remaining water. Stir in the soy sauce and rice wine or sherry.

6 Add the mixture to the sauce and bring to the boil, stirring until it thickens and becomes glossy. Add all the vegetables, the chopped pickles and the pickle liquid and cook over a gentle heat for 2 minutes.

7 Using the foil strips as a support, carefully transfer the cooked fish to a platter, then ease the foil away. Spoon the warm sauce over the fish and serve.

1 Rinse the fish inside and out. Dry with kitchen paper. Create a support for each fish by placing a broad strip of oiled foil on the work surface. Place the fish on the foil. Mix the ginger, spring onions and salt, then tuck the mixture into the body cavity.

4 Meanwhile, prepare the sauce. Drain the chow chow in a sieve (strainer) placed over a bowl and reserve the liquid. Cut each of the pickles in half. Pour 250ml/8fl oz/1 cup of the water into a pan and bring to the boil. Add the vinegar and sugar and stir until dissolved.

COOK'S TIP

If using one large fish that is too long to fit in a fish kettle, cut it in half and cook it on a rack placed over a large roasting pan. Pour in a similar quantity of boiling water as for the fish kettle, cover with foil and cook on top of the stove. Allow about 20–25 minutes for a 1kg/2¼ lb fish; 15–20 minutes for a 675g/1½lb fish. Reassemble the halved fish before coating it with the sauce.

Per portion: Energy 156Kcal/655kJ; Protein 19.1g; Carbohydrate 7.8g, of which sugars 6.3g; Fat 5.1g, of which saturates 1g; Cholesterol 67mg; Calcium 77mg; Fibre 2.4g; Sodium 739mg.

FILLETS OF TURBOT WITH OYSTERS

THIS LUXURIOUS DISH IS PERFECT FOR SPECIAL OCCASIONS. IT IS WORTH BUYING A WHOLE TURBOT AND ASKING THE FISHMONGER TO FILLET AND SKIN IT FOR YOU. KEEP THE HEAD, BONES AND TRIMMINGS FOR STOCK. SOLE, BRILL AND HALIBUT CAN ALL BE SUBSTITUTED FOR THE TURBOT.

SERVES FOUR

INGREDIENTS

   12 Pacific (rock) oysters
   115g/4oz/½ cup butter
   2 carrots, cut into julienne strips
   200g/7oz celeriac, cut into
     julienne strips
   the white parts of 2 leeks, cut into
     julienne strips
   375ml/13fl oz/generous 1½ cups
     Champagne or dry white sparkling
     wine (about ½ bottle)
   105ml/7 tbsp whipping cream
   1 turbot, about 1.75kg/4–4½lb,
     filleted and skinned
   salt and ground white pepper

1 Using an oyster knife, open the oysters over a bowl to catch the juices, then carefully remove them from their shells, discarding the shells, and place them in a separate bowl. Set aside until required.

2 Melt 25g/1oz/2 tbsp of the butter in a shallow pan, add the vegetable julienne and cook over a low heat until tender but not coloured. Pour in half the Champagne or sparkling wine and cook very gently until all the liquid has evaporated. Keep the heat low so that the vegetables do not colour.

3 Strain the oyster juices into a small pan and add the cream and the remaining Champagne or sparkling wine. Place over a medium heat until the mixture has reduced to the consistency of thin cream. Dice half the remaining butter and whisk it into the sauce, one piece at a time, until smooth. Season to taste, then pour the sauce into a blender and process until velvety smooth.

4 Return the sauce to the pan, bring it to just below boiling point, then drop in the oysters. Poach for about 1 minute, to warm but barely cook. Keep warm, but do not let the sauce boil.

5 Season the turbot fillets with salt and pepper. Heat the remaining butter in a large frying pan until foaming, then cook the fillets over a medium heat for about 2–3 minutes on each side, until cooked through and golden.

6 Cut each turbot fillet into three pieces and arrange on individual warmed plates. Pile the vegetable julienne on top, place three oysters around the turbot fillets on each plate and pour the sauce around the edge.

Per portion: Energy 752Kcal/3125kJ; Protein 66.7g; Carbohydrate 9.2g, of which sugars 8g; Fat 44.1g, of which saturates 23.9g; Cholesterol 106mg; Calcium 252mg; Fibre 1.4g; Sodium 370mg.

YUCATAN-STYLE SHARK STEAK

A FIRM-FLESHED FISH, SHARK IS WIDELY AVAILABLE, EITHER FRESH OR FROZEN. IT NEEDS CAREFUL WATCHING, AS OVERCOOKING WILL MAKE IT DRY AND TOUGH, BUT THE FLAVOUR IS EXCELLENT.

SERVES FOUR

INGREDIENTS

 grated rind and juice of 1 orange
 juice of 1 small lime
 45ml/3 tbsp white wine
 30ml/2 tbsp olive oil
 2 garlic cloves, crushed
 10ml/2 tsp ground achiote seed
  (annatto powder)
 2.5ml/½ tsp cayenne pepper
 2.5ml/½ tsp dried marjoram
 5ml/1 tsp salt
 4 shark steaks
 fresh oregano leaves, to garnish
 4 wheat-flour tortillas and any
  suitable salsa, to serve

COOK'S TIP

Shark freezes successfully, with little or no loss of flavour on thawing, so use frozen steaks if you can't find fresh.

1 Put the orange rind and juice in a shallow non-metallic dish which is large enough to hold all the shark steaks in a single layer. Add the lime juice, white wine, olive oil, garlic, ground achiote, cayenne, marjoram and salt. Mix well.

2 Add the shark steaks to the dish and spoon the marinade over them. Cover and set aside for 1 hour, turning once.

3 Heat a griddle pan until very hot and cook the marinated shark steaks for 2–3 minutes on each side. Alternatively, they are very good cooked on the barbecue, as long as they are cooked after the coals have lost their fierce initial heat. Do not overcook.

4 Garnish the shark steaks with oregano and serve with the tortillas and salsa. A green vegetable would also go well.

Per portion: Energy 239Kcal/1006kJ; Protein 40.6g; Carbohydrate 0.7g, of which sugars 0.1g; Fat 7.5g, of which saturates 1.2g; Cholesterol 77mg; Calcium 33mg; Fibre 0.2g; Sodium 246mg.

BAKED SEA BREAM WITH TOMATOES

JOHN DORY, TURBOT OR SEA BASS CAN ALL BE COOKED THIS WAY. IF YOU PREFER TO USE FILLETED FISH, CHOOSE A CHUNKY FILLET, LIKE COD, AND BAKE IT SKIN SIDE UP. ROASTING THE TOMATOES BRINGS OUT THEIR SWEETNESS, WHICH CONTRASTS BEAUTIFULLY WITH THE FLAVOUR OF THE FISH.

2 Meanwhile, cut the potatoes into 1cm/½in slices. Par-boil for 5 minutes. Drain and set aside.

3 Grease an ovenproof dish with oil. Arrange the potatoes in a single layer with the lemon slices over; sprinkle on the bay leaf, thyme and basil. Season and drizzle with half the remaining olive oil. Lay the fish on top, season; pour over the wine and the rest of the oil. Arrange the tomatoes around the fish.

4 Mix together the breadcrumbs, garlic and parsley and sprinkle over the fish. Bake for 30 minutes, until the flesh comes away easily from the bone. Garnish with chopped parsley or basil.

SERVES FOUR TO SIX

INGREDIENTS

  8 ripe tomatoes
  10ml/2 tsp caster (superfine) sugar
  200ml/7fl oz/scant 1 cup olive oil
  450g/1lb new potatoes
  1 lemon, sliced
  1 bay leaf
  1 fresh thyme sprig
  8 fresh basil leaves
  1 sea bream, about 900g–1kg/
    2–2¼lb, cleaned and scaled
  150ml/¼ pint/⅔ cup dry white wine
  30ml/2 tbsp fresh white breadcrumbs
  2 garlic cloves, crushed
  15ml/1 tbsp finely chopped
    fresh parsley
  salt and ground black pepper
  fresh flat parsley or basil leaves,
    chopped, to garnish

1 Preheat the oven to 240°C/475°F/ Gas 9. Using a sharp knife, cut the tomatoes in half lengthways and arrange them in a single layer in a large, ovenproof dish, cut side up. Sprinkle with the caster sugar, season to taste with salt and pepper and drizzle over a little of the olive oil. Roast for 30–40 minutes, until the tomatoes are soft and lightly browned on top.

Per portion: Energy 571Kcal/2383kJ; Protein 25.9g; Carbohydrate 29.4g, of which sugars 7.2g; Fat 37.1g, of which saturates 4.9g; Cholesterol 48mg; Calcium 82mg; Fibre 3g; Sodium 224mg.

FILLETS OF BRILL IN RED WINE SAUCE

FORGET THE OLD MAXIM THAT RED WINE AND FISH DO NOT GO WELL TOGETHER. THE ROBUST SAUCE ADDS COLOUR AND RICHNESS TO THIS EXCELLENT DISH. TURBOT, HALIBUT AND JOHN DORY ARE ALSO GOOD COOKED THIS WAY.

SERVES FOUR

INGREDIENTS

    4 brill fillets, about 175–200g/6–7oz
      each, skinned
    150g/5oz/⅔ cup chilled butter,
      diced, plus extra for greasing
    115g/4oz shallots, thinly sliced
    200ml/7fl oz/scant 1 cup robust
      red wine
    200ml/7fl oz/scant 1 cup fish stock
    salt and ground white pepper
    fresh chervil or flat leaf parsley
      leaves, to garnish

3 Using a fish slice or metal spatula, carefully lift the fish and shallots on to a serving dish, cover with foil and keep hot.

4 Transfer the dish to the hob (stovetop) and bring the cooking liquid to the boil over a high heat. Cook it until it has reduced by half. Lower the heat and whisk in the chilled butter, one piece at a time, to make a smooth, shiny sauce. Season with salt and ground white pepper, set aside and keep hot.

5 Divide the shallots among four warmed plates and lay the brill fillets on top. Pour the sauce over and around the fish and garnish with the chervil or flat leaf parsley.

1 Preheat the oven to 180°C/350°F/ Gas 4. Season the fish on both sides with salt and pepper. Generously butter a flameproof dish, which is large enough to take all the brill fillets in a single layer without overlapping. Spread the shallots over the base and lay the fish fillets on top. Season.

2 Pour in the red wine and fish stock, cover the dish and bring the liquid to just below boiling point. Transfer the dish to the oven and bake for 6–8 minutes, until just cooked.

Per portion: Energy 511Kcal/2123kJ; Protein 35.7g; Carbohydrate 1.3g, of which sugars 1.3g; Fat 36.7g, of which saturates 19.5g; Cholesterol 156mg; Calcium 97mg; Fibre 0.4g; Sodium 454mg.

BAKED SALMON WITH WATERCRESS SAUCE

WHOLE BAKED SALMON IS A CLASSIC DISH SERVED AT WEDDING PARTIES AND JUST ABOUT ANY OTHER BIG OCCASION. BAKING THE SALMON IN FOIL PRODUCES A FLESH RATHER LIKE THAT OF A POACHED FISH BUT WITH THE EASE OF BAKING. DECORATING THE FISH WITH THIN SLICES OF CUCUMBER LOOKS PRETTY AND WILL CONCEAL ANY FLESH THAT MAY LOOK RAGGED AFTER SKINNING.

SERVES SIX TO EIGHT

INGREDIENTS

2–3kg/4½–6¾lb salmon, cleaned, with head and tail left on
3–5 spring onions (scallions), thinly sliced
1 lemon, thinly sliced
1 cucumber, thinly sliced
fresh dill sprigs, to garnish
lemon wedges, to serve
For the watercress sauce
3 garlic cloves, chopped
200g/7oz watercress leaves, finely chopped
40g/1½oz fresh tarragon, finely chopped
300g/11oz mayonnaise
15–30ml/1–2 tbsp freshly squeezed lemon juice
200g/7oz/scant 1 cup unsalted (sweet) butter
salt and ground black pepper

1 Preheat the oven to 180°C/350°F/Gas 4. Rinse the salmon and lay it on a large piece of foil. Stuff the fish cavity with the sliced spring onions and layer the lemon slices inside and around the fish, then sprinkle with plenty of salt and ground black pepper.

2 Loosely fold the foil around the fish and fold the edges over to seal. Bake for about 1 hour.

3 Remove the fish from the oven and leave to stand, still wrapped in the foil, for about 15 minutes, then unwrap the parcel and leave the fish to cool.

4 When the fish is cool, carefully lift it on to a large plate, still covered with lemon slices. Cover the fish tightly with clear film (plastic wrap) and chill for several hours.

5 Before serving, discard the lemon slices around the fish. Using a blunt knife to lift up the edge of the skin, carefully peel the skin away from the flesh, avoiding tearing the flesh, and pull out any fins at the same time.

6 Arrange the cucumber slices in overlapping rows along the length of the fish, to resemble large fish scales.

COOK'S TIP
Do not prepare the sauce more than a few hours ahead of serving as the watercress will discolour it.

7 To make the sauce, put the garlic, watercress, tarragon, mayonnaise and lemon juice in a food processor or blender or a bowl, and process or mix to combine.

8 Melt the butter, then add to the watercress mixture, a little at a time, processing or stirring, until the butter has been incorporated and the sauce is thick and smooth. Cover and chill before serving. Serve the fish, garnished with dill, with the sauce and lemon wedges.

VARIATION
Instead of cooking a whole fish, prepare 6–8 salmon steaks. Place each fish steak on an individual square of foil, then top with a slice of onion and a slice of lemon and season generously with salt and ground black pepper. Loosely wrap the foil up around the fish, fold the edges to seal and place the parcels on a baking sheet. Bake as above for 10–15 minutes, or until the flesh is opaque. Serve cold with watercress sauce, garnished with slices of cucumber.

Salmon <u>with</u> Tequila Cream Sauce

Use reposada tequila, which is lightly aged, for this sauce. It has a smoother, more rounded flavour, which goes well with the cream.

SERVES FOUR

INGREDIENTS

  3 fresh jalapeño chillies
  45ml/3 tbsp olive oil
  1 small onion, finely chopped
  150ml/¼ pint/⅔ cup fish stock
  grated rind and juice of 1 lime
  120ml/4fl oz/½ cup single
   (light) cream
  30ml/2 tbsp reposada tequila
  1 firm avocado
  4 salmon fillets
  salt and ground white pepper
  strips of green (bell) pepper

1 Roast the chillies in a frying pan until the skins are blistered, being careful not to let the flesh burn. Put them in a strong plastic bag and tie the top to keep the steam in. Set aside for 20 minutes.

2 Heat 15ml/1 tbsp of the oil in a pan. Cook the onion for 3–4 minutes, then add the stock, lime rind and juice. Cook for 10 minutes, until the stock starts to reduce. Remove the chillies from the bag and peel off the skins, slit them and scrape out the seeds.

3 Stir the cream into the onion and stock mixture. Slice the chilli flesh into strips and add to the pan. Cook over a gentle heat, stirring constantly, for 2–3 minutes. Season to taste with salt and white pepper.

4 Stir the tequila into the onion and chilli mixture. Leave the pan over a very low heat. Peel the avocado, remove the stone (pit) and slice the flesh. Brush the salmon fillets on one side with a little of the remaining oil.

5 Heat a frying pan or ridged griddle pan until very hot and add the salmon, oiled side down. Cook for 2–3 minutes, until the underside is golden, then brush the top with oil, turn each fillet over and cook the other side until the fish is cooked and flakes easily when tested with the tip of a sharp knife.

6 Serve the fish on a pool of sauce, with the avocado slices. Garnish with strips of green pepper and fresh flat leaf parsley, if you like.

Per portion: Energy 445Kcal/1846kJ; Protein 27.1g; Carbohydrate 2.5g, of which sugars 1.7g; Fat 34.8g, of which saturates 8.7g; Cholesterol 79mg; Calcium 61mg; Fibre 1.5g; Sodium 68mg.

ROAST MONKFISH WITH GARLIC

MONKFISH TIED UP AND COOKED IN THIS WAY IS KNOWN IN FRENCH AS A "GIGOT", BECAUSE IT RESEMBLES A LEG OF LAMB. THE COMBINATION OF MONKFISH AND GARLIC IS SUPERB. FOR A CONTRAST IN COLOUR, SERVE IT WITH VIBRANT GREEN BEANS.

SERVES FOUR TO SIX

INGREDIENTS

1kg/2¼lb monkfish tail, skinned
14 fat garlic cloves
5ml/1 tsp fresh thyme leaves
30ml/2 tbsp olive oil
juice of 1 lemon
2 bay leaves
salt and ground black pepper

1 Preheat the oven to 220°C/425°F/ Gas 7. Remove any membrane from the monkfish tail and cut out the central bone. Peel two garlic cloves and cut them into thin slivers. Sprinkle a quarter of these and half the thyme leaves over the cut side of the fish, then close it up and use fine kitchen string to tie it into a neat shape, like a boned piece of meat. Pat dry with kitchen paper.

2 Make incisions on either side of the fish and push in the remaining garlic slivers. Heat half the olive oil in a frying pan which can safely be used in the oven. When the oil is hot, put in the monkfish and brown it all over for about 5 minutes, until evenly coloured. Season with salt and pepper, sprinkle with lemon juice and then sprinkle over the remaining thyme.

3 Tuck the bay leaves under the monkfish, arrange the remaining (unpeeled) garlic cloves around it and drizzle the remaining olive oil over the fish and the garlic. Transfer the frying pan to the oven and roast the monkfish for 20–25 minutes, until the flesh is cooked through.

4 Place on a warmed serving dish with the garlic and some green beans. To serve, remove the string and cut the monkfish into 2cm/¾in thick slices.

COOK'S TIPS
• The garlic heads can be used whole.
• When serving the monkfish, invite each guest to pop out the soft garlic pulp with a fork and spread it over the monkfish.
• Use two smaller monkfish tails.

Per portion: Energy 253Kcal/1065kJ; Protein 45.2g; Carbohydrate 3.1g, of which sugars 0.3g; Fat 6.6g, of which saturates 1.1g; Cholesterol 40mg; Calcium 26mg; Fibre 0.8g; Sodium 51mg.

SHELLFISH

This chapter includes an array of ideas for soups, pasta and stews, with the recipes featuring a variety of shellfish from mussels, clams and lobster to octopus and squid. For a memorable dinner party meal, try the stylish Crab Cakes, delicious Seared Scallops with Chive Sauce on Leek and Carrot Rice, or an impressive and filling Seafood Paella.

CRAB CAKES

Unlike fish cakes, crab cakes are bound with egg and mayonnaise or tartare sauce instead of potatoes, which makes them light in texture. If you prefer, they can be grilled instead of fried; brush with a little oil first.

SERVES FOUR

INGREDIENTS
450g/1lb mixed brown and white
  crab meat
30ml/2 tbsp mayonnaise or
  tartare sauce
2.5–5ml/½–1 tsp mustard powder
1 egg, lightly beaten
Tabasco sauce
45ml/3 tbsp chopped
  fresh parsley
4 spring onions (scallions), finely
  chopped (optional)
50–75g/2–3oz/½–¾ cup dried
  breadcrumbs, preferably home-made
sunflower oil, for frying
salt, ground black pepper and
  cayenne pepper
chopped spring onions (scallions),
  to garnish
red onion marmalade, to serve

1 Put the crab meat in a bowl and stir in the mayonnaise or tartare sauce, with the mustard and egg. Season with Tabasco, salt, pepper and cayenne.

2 Stir in the parsley, spring onions, if using, and 50g/2oz/½ cup of the breadcrumbs. The mixture should be just firm enough to hold together; depending on how much brown crab meat there is, you may need to add some more breadcrumbs.

3 Divide the mixture into eight portions, roll each into a ball and flatten slightly to make a thick flat disc. Spread out the crab cakes on a platter and put in the refrigerator for 30 minutes before frying.

4 Pour the oil into a shallow pan to a depth of about 5mm/¼in. Cook the crab cakes, in two batches, until golden brown all over. Drain on kitchen paper and keep hot. Serve with a spring onion garnish and red onion marmalade.

Per portion: Energy 285Kcal/1187kJ; Protein 23.9g; Carbohydrate 10.3g, of which sugars 0.9g; Fat 16.7g, of which saturates 2.4g; Cholesterol 134mg; Calcium 178mg; Fibre 0.8g; Sodium 768mg.

VEGETABLE-STUFFED SQUID

SHIRLEY CONRAN FAMOUSLY SAID THAT LIFE IS TOO SHORT TO STUFF A MUSHROOM. THE SAME MIGHT BE SAID OF SQUID, EXCEPT THAT THE RESULT IS SO DELICIOUS THAT IT MAKES THE EFFORT SEEM WORTHWHILE. SMALL CUTTLEFISH CAN BE PREPARED IN THE SAME WAY. SERVE WITH SAFFRON RICE.

SERVES FOUR

INGREDIENTS

4 medium squid, or 12 small squid,
  skinned and cleaned
75g/3oz/6 tbsp butter
50g/2oz/1 cup fresh
  white breadcrumbs
2 shallots, chopped
4 garlic cloves, chopped
1 leek, thinly diced
2 carrots, finely diced
150ml/¼ pint/⅔ cup fish stock
30ml/2 tbsp olive oil
30ml/2 tbsp chopped fresh parsley
salt and ground black pepper
fresh rosemary sprigs, to garnish
saffron rice, to serve

3 Heat half the olive oil in the frying pan, add the chopped squid and cook over a high heat for 1 minute. Remove the squid with a slotted spoon and stir into the vegetables. Stir in the parsley.

4 Put the stuffing mixture into a piping (pastry) bag or use a teaspoon to stuff the squid tubes with the mixture. Do not overfill them, as the stuffing will swell lightly during cooking. Secure the openings with cocktail sticks (toothpicks) or sew up with fine thread.

5 Heat the remaining olive oil in the frying pan, place the stuffed squid in the pan and cook until they are sealed on all sides and golden brown. Transfer the frying pan to the oven and roast the squid for 20 minutes.

6 Unless the squid are very small, carefully cut them into three or four slices and arrange on a bed of saffron rice. Spoon the cooking juices over the squid and serve immediately, garnished with sprigs of rosemary.

1 Preheat the oven to 220°C/425°F/ Gas 7. Cut off the tentacles and side flaps from the squid and chop these finely. Set the squid aside. Melt half the butter in a large frying pan that can safely be used in the oven. Add the fresh white breadcrumbs and cook until they are golden brown, stirring to prevent them from burning. Transfer the breadcrumbs to a bowl and set aside until required.

2 Heat the remaining butter in the frying pan and add the chopped and diced vegetables. Cook until softened but not browned, then stir in the fish stock and cook until it has reduced and the vegetables are very soft. Season to taste with salt and ground black pepper and transfer to the bowl with the breadcrumbs. Mix lightly together.

Per portion: Energy 356Kcal/1486kJ; Protein 21.8g; Carbohydrate 15.2g, of which sugars 3.6g; Fat 23.6g, of which saturates 11.1g; Cholesterol 321mg; Calcium 55mg; Fibre 1.9g; Sodium 352mg.

SEARED SCALLOPS WITH CHIVE SAUCE ON LEEK AND CARROT RICE

SCALLOPS ARE ONE OF THE MOST DELICIOUS SHELLFISH. HERE THEY ARE PARTNERED WITH A DELICATE CHIVE SAUCE AND A PILAFF OF WILD AND WHITE RICE WITH SWEET LEEKS AND CARROTS.

SERVES FOUR

INGREDIENTS
12–16 shelled scallops
45ml/3 tbsp olive oil
50g/2oz/⅓ cup wild rice
65g/2½ oz/5 tbsp butter
4 carrots, cut into long thin strips
2 leeks, cut into thick,
  diagonal slices
1 small onion, finely chopped
115g/4oz/⅔ cup long grain rice
1 fresh bay leaf
200ml/7fl oz/scant 1 cup white wine
450ml/¾ pint/scant 2 cups fish stock
60ml/4 tbsp double (heavy) cream
a little lemon juice
25ml/5 tsp chopped fresh chives
30ml/2 tbsp fresh chervil sprigs
salt and ground black pepper

1 Lightly season the scallops, brush with 15ml/1 tbsp of the olive oil and set aside.

2 Cook the wild rice in plenty of boiling water for about 30 minutes, until tender, then drain well.

3 Melt half the butter in a small frying pan and cook the carrots over a low heat for 4–5 minutes. Add the leeks and cook for a further 2 minutes. Season with salt and pepper and add 30–45ml/ 2–3 tbsp water, then cover and cook for a few minutes more. Uncover and cook until the liquid has reduced. Remove from the heat and set aside.

4 Melt half the rest of the butter with 15ml/1 tbsp of the remaining oil in a heavy pan. Add the onion and cook over a low heat for 3–4 minutes, until softened but not browned.

5 Add the long grain rice and bay leaf and cook, stirring constantly, until the rice looks translucent and the grains are coated with oil.

6 Pour in half the wine and half the stock. Season with 2.5ml/½ tsp salt and bring to the boil. Stir, then cover and cook very gently for 15 minutes, or until the liquid is absorbed and the rice is cooked and tender.

7 Reheat the carrots and leeks gently, then stir them into the long grain rice with the wild rice. Add seasoning to taste, if necessary.

8 Meanwhile, pour the remaining wine and stock into a small pan and boil rapidly until reduced by half.

COOK'S TIP
Choose fresh, rather than frozen, scallops as the frozen ones tend to exude water on cooking. Scallops need only the briefest cooking at high heat, just until they turn opaque and brown on each side, so have the pan very hot. Although some people avoid eating the orange-coloured coral, it is delicious and many people consider it to be the best part.

9 Heat a heavy frying pan over a high heat. Add the remaining butter and oil. Sear the scallops for 1–2 minutes on each side. Set aside and keep warm.

10 Pour the reduced stock into the pan and heat until bubbling, then add the cream and boil until thickened. Season with lemon juice, salt and pepper. Stir in the chives and scallops.

11 Stir the chervil into the rice and pile it on to plates. Arrange the scallops on top and spoon the sauce over the rice.

Per portion: Energy 482Kcal/2014kJ; Protein 28.1g; Carbohydrate 42.7g, of which sugars 6g; Fat 18.6g, of which saturates 6.7g; Cholesterol 68mg; Calcium 80mg; Fibre 3g; Sodium 200mg.

Moules Provençale

Eating these delectable mussels is a messy affair, which is part of their charm. Hand round plenty of crusty French bread for mopping up the juices and don't forget fingerbowls of warm water and a plate for discarded shells.

SERVES FOUR

INGREDIENTS
30ml/2 tbsp olive oil
200g/7oz rindless unsmoked streaky (fatty) bacon, cubed
1 onion, finely chopped
3 garlic cloves, finely chopped
1 bay leaf
15ml/1 tbsp chopped fresh mixed Provençal herbs, such as thyme, marjoram, basil, oregano and savory
15–30ml/1–2 tbsp sun-dried tomatoes in oil, chopped
4 large, very ripe tomatoes, peeled, seeded and chopped
50g/2oz/½ cup pitted black olives, chopped
105ml/7 tbsp dry white wine
2.25kg/5–5¼lb fresh mussels, scrubbed and bearded
salt and ground black pepper
60ml/4 tbsp coarsely chopped fresh parsley, to garnish

1 Heat the oil in a large pan. Cook the bacon until golden and crisp. Remove with a slotted spoon; set aside. Add the onion and garlic to the pan and cook gently until softened. Add the herbs, with both types of tomatoes. Cook gently for 5 minutes, stirring frequently. Stir in the olives and season.

2 Put the wine and mussels in another pan. Cover and shake over a high heat for 5 minutes, until the mussels open. Discard any that remain closed.

3 Strain the mussel cooking liquid into the pan containing the tomato sauce through a sieve lined with muslin (cheesecloth) and boil until the mixture is reduced by about one-third. Add the mussels and stir to coat them thoroughly with the sauce. Remove and discard the bay leaf.

4 Divide the mussels and sauce among four heated dishes. Sprinkle over the fried bacon and chopped parsley and serve piping hot.

Per portion: Energy 439Kcal/1836kJ; Protein 34.9g; Carbohydrate 12.8g, of which sugars 6.9g; Fat 25.9g, of which saturates 6.2g; Cholesterol 123mg; Calcium 112mg; Fibre 2.4g; Sodium 1467mg.

FRENCH MUSSELS

THIS IS A TRADITIONAL DISH OF MUSSELS COOKED WITH SHALLOTS, GARLIC AND SAFFRON FROM THE WEST ATLANTIC COAST OF FRANCE. IT TASTES AS SUPERB AS IT LOOKS.

SERVES SIX

INGREDIENTS

2kg/4½lb fresh mussels, scrubbed
  and bearded
250g/9oz shallots, finely chopped
300ml/½ pint/1¼ cups medium white
  wine, such as Vouvray
generous pinch of saffron threads
  (about 12 strands)
75g/3oz/6 tbsp butter
2 celery sticks, finely chopped
5ml/1 tsp fennel seeds,
  lightly crushed
2 large garlic cloves, finely chopped
250ml/8fl oz/1 cup fish or stock
1 bay leaf
pinch of cayenne pepper
2 large (US extra large) egg yolks
150ml/¼ pint/⅔ cup double
  (heavy) cream
juice of ½–1 lemon
30–45ml/2–3 tbsp chopped
  fresh parsley
salt and ground black pepper

1 Discard any mussels that do not shut when tapped sharply.

2 Place 30ml/2 tbsp of the shallots with the wine in a wide pan and bring to the boil. Add half the mussels and cover, then boil rapidly for 1 minute, shaking the pan once. Remove all the mussels, discarding any that remain closed. Repeat with the remaining mussels. Remove the top half-shell from each mussel. Strain the cooking liquid through a fine sieve into a bowl and stir in the saffron, then set aside.

3 Melt 50g/2oz/4 tbsp of the butter in a heavy pan. Add the remaining shallots and celery and cook over a low heat, stirring occasionally, for 5–6 minutes, until softened but not browned. Add the fennel seeds and half of the garlic, then cook for another 2–3 minutes.

4 Pour in the reserved mussel liquid, bring to the boil and then simmer for 5 minutes before adding the stock, bay leaf and cayenne. Season with salt and pepper to taste, then simmer, uncovered, for 5–10 minutes.

5 Beat the egg yolks with the cream, then whisk in a ladleful of the hot liquid followed by the juice of ½ lemon. Whisk this mixture back into the sauce. Cook over a very low heat, without allowing it to boil, for 5–10 minutes until slightly thickened. Taste for seasoning and add more lemon juice if necessary.

6 Stir the remaining garlic, butter and most of the parsley into the sauce with the mussels and reheat for 30–60 seconds. Distribute the mussels among six soup plates and ladle the sauce over. Sprinkle with the remaining parsley and serve.

Per portion: Energy 568Kcal/2360kJ; Protein 26g; Carbohydrate 9.9g, of which sugars 5.4g; Fat 42.1g, of which saturates 23.6g; Cholesterol 272mg; Calcium 149mg; Fibre 1.4g; Sodium 632mg.

LOBSTER RAVIOLI

IT IS ESSENTIAL TO USE HOME-MADE PASTA TO OBTAIN THE DELICACY AND THINNESS THAT THIS SUPERB FILLING DESERVES. BEFORE YOU START THE RECIPE, MAKE A WELL-FLAVOURED FISH STOCK, USING THE LOBSTER SHELL AND HEAD.

SERVES FOUR

INGREDIENTS
1 lobster, about 450g/1lb, cooked
   and taken out of the shell
2 soft white bread slices, about
   50g/2oz, crusts removed
200ml/7fl oz/scant 1 cup fish stock
1 egg
250ml/8fl oz/1 cup double
   (heavy) cream
15ml/1 tbsp chopped fresh chives,
   plus extra to garnish
15ml/1 tbsp finely chopped
   fresh chervil
salt and ground white pepper
fresh chives, to garnish
For the pasta dough
   225g/8oz/2 cups strong white
      bread flour
   2 eggs, plus 2 egg yolks
For the mushroom sauce
   a large pinch of saffron threads
   25g/1oz/2 tbsp butter
   2 shallots, finely chopped
   200g/7oz/3 cups button (white)
      mushrooms, finely chopped
   juice of ½ lemon
   200ml/7fl oz/scant 1 cup
      double (heavy) cream

1 Make the pasta dough. Sift the flour with a pinch of salt. Put into a food processor with the eggs and yolks and process until the mixture resembles breadcrumbs. Turn out on to a floured surface; knead to a smooth dough. Wrap in clear film (plastic wrap) and leave to rest in the refrigerator for 1 hour.

2 Meanwhile, make the lobster filling. Cut the lobster meat into large chunks and place in a bowl. Tear the white bread into small pieces and soak them in 45ml/3 tbsp of the fish stock. Place in a food processor with half the egg and 30–45ml/2–3 tbsp of the double cream and process until smooth. Stir the mixture into the lobster meat, then add the chives and chervil and season to taste with salt and white pepper.

3 Roll the ravioli dough to a thickness of 3mm/⅛in, preferably using a pasta machine. The process can be done by hand with a rolling pin but is quite hard work. Divide the dough into four rectangles and dust each rectangle lightly with flour.

4 Spoon six equal heaps of filling on to one sheet of pasta, leaving about 3cm/1¼in between each pile of filling. Lightly beat the remaining egg with a tablespoon of water and brush it over the pasta between the piles of filling. Cover with a second sheet of pasta. Repeat with the other two sheets of pasta and remaining filling.

5 Using your fingertips, press the top layer of dough down well between the piles of filling, making sure each is well sealed. Cut between the heaps with a 7.5cm/3in fluted pastry cutter or a pasta wheel to make twelve ravioli.

6 Place the ravioli in a single layer on a baking sheet, cover with clear film or a damp cloth, and put in the refrigerator while you make the sauces.

7 Make the mushroom sauce. Soak the saffron in 15ml/1 tbsp warm water. Melt the butter in a pan and cook the shallots over a low heat until they are soft but not coloured.

8 Add the chopped mushrooms and lemon juice and continue to cook over a low heat until almost all the liquid has evaporated. Stir in the saffron, with its soaking water, and the cream, then cook gently, stirring occasionally, until the sauce has thickened. Keep warm while you cook the ravioli.

Per portion: Energy 652Kcal/2722kJ; Protein 23g; Carbohydrate 52.2g, of which sugars 3.1g; Fat 40.5g, of which saturates 22.2g; Cholesterol 361mg; Calcium 186mg; Fibre 2.9g; Sodium 298mg.

9 In another pan, bring the remaining fish stock to the boil, stir in the rest of the cream and bubble to make a slightly thickened sauce. Season to taste with salt and pepper and keep warm. Bring a large pan of lightly salted water to a rolling boil. Gently drop in the ravioli (left) and cook for 3–4 minutes, until the pasta is just tender.

10 Place three ravioli on to the centre of each of four individual warmed plates, spoon over a little of the mushroom sauce and pour a ribbon of fish sauce around the edge. Serve immediately, garnished with chopped and whole fresh chives.

CLAMS WITH NEAPOLITAN TOMATO SAUCE

THIS RECIPE TAKES ITS NAME FROM THE CITY OF NAPLES, WHERE BOTH FRESH TOMATO SAUCE AND SHELLFISH ARE TRADITIONALLY SERVED WITH VERMICELLI. HERE THE TWO ARE COMBINED TO MAKE A VERY TASTY DISH THAT IS PERFECT FOR A COLD WINTER'S EVENING.

SERVES FOUR

INGREDIENTS
  1kg/2¼lb fresh clams
  250ml/8fl oz/1 cup dry white wine,
    or vegetable stock
  2 garlic cloves, bruised
  1 large handful fresh flat leaf parsley
  30ml/2 tbsp extra virgin olive oil or
    sunflower oil
  1 small onion, finely chopped
  8 ripe plum tomatoes, peeled, seeded
    and finely chopped
  ½–1 fresh red chilli, seeded and
    finely chopped
  350g/12oz dried vermicelli
  salt and ground black pepper

1 Scrub the clams thoroughly with a brush under cold running water and discard any that are open or do not close their shells when sharply tapped against the work surface.

2 Pour the white wine or vegetable stock into a large, heavy pan and add the bruised garlic cloves. Shred half the parsley finely, add to the wine or stock, then add the clams.

3 Cover the pan tightly with the lid and bring to the boil over a high heat. Cook for about 5 minutes, shaking the pan frequently, until the clams have opened.

4 Turn the clams into a large colander set over a bowl and let the liquid drain through. Leave the clams until cool enough to handle, then remove about two-thirds of them from their shells, adding the clam liquor to the bowl of cooking liquid. Discard any clams that have failed to open.

5 Set both shelled and unshelled clams aside, keeping the unshelled clams warm in a bowl covered with a lid or thick cloth.

6 Heat the oil in a pan, add the onion and cook gently, stirring frequently, for about 5 minutes, until softened and lightly coloured. Add the tomatoes, then strain in the clam cooking liquid. Add the chilli, and salt and pepper to taste.

7 Bring to the boil, half cover the pan and simmer gently for 15–20 minutes. Meanwhile, cook the pasta according to the packet instructions. Chop the remaining parsley finely.

8 Add the shelled clams to the tomato sauce, stir well and heat through very gently for 2–3 minutes.

9 Drain the cooked pasta well and tip it into a warmed bowl. Taste the sauce for seasoning, then pour the sauce over the pasta and toss everything together well. Garnish with the reserved clams, sprinkle the parsley over the pasta and serve immediately.

Per portion: Energy 500Kcal/2091kJ; Protein 21.6g; Carbohydrate 77.3g, of which sugars 6.9g; Fat 7.1g, of which saturates 1.1g; Cholesterol 50mg; Calcium 134mg; Fibre 2.9g; Sodium 932mg.

PASTA WITH TOMATOES AND SHELLFISH

COLOURFUL AND DELICIOUS, THIS TYPICAL GENOESE DISH IS IDEAL FOR A DINNER PARTY. THE TOMATO SAUCE IS QUITE RUNNY, SO SERVE IT WITH CRUSTY BREAD AND SPOONS AS WELL AS FORKS. FOR A REAL TASTE OF ITALY, CHOOSE A DRY WHITE ITALIAN WINE TO SERVE WITH THE MEAL.

SERVES FOUR

INGREDIENTS
45ml/3 tbsp olive oil
1 small onion, chopped
1 garlic clove, crushed
½ fresh red chilli, seeded
  and chopped
200g/7oz can chopped
  plum tomatoes
30ml/2 tbsp chopped fresh flat
  leaf parsley
400g/14oz fresh clams
400g/14oz fresh mussels
60ml/4 tbsp dry white wine
400g/14oz/3½ cups dried trenette
  or spaghetti
a few fresh basil leaves
90g/3½oz/⅔ cup cooked, peeled
  prawns (shrimp), thawed and
  thoroughly dried if frozen
salt and ground black pepper
lemon wedges and chopped fresh herbs,
  such as parsley or thyme, to garnish

1 Heat 30ml/2tbsp of the oil in a frying pan or medium pan. Add the onion, garlic and chilli and cook over a medium heat for 1–2 minutes, stirring constantly. Stir in the tomatoes, half the parsley and pepper to taste. Bring to the boil, lower the heat, cover and simmer for 15 minutes.

2 Meanwhile, scrub the clams and mussels under cold running water. Discard any that are open and that do not close when sharply tapped against the work surface.

3 In a large pan, heat the remaining oil. Add the clams and mussels, with the rest of the parsley and toss over a high heat for a few seconds. Pour in the wine, then cover tightly. Cook for about 5 minutes, shaking the pan frequently, until the clams and mussels have opened.

4 Transfer the clams and mussels to a bowl, discarding any shellfish that have failed to open. Strain the cooking liquid and set aside. Reserve eight clams and four mussels for the garnish, then remove the rest from their shells.

5 Cook the pasta according to the instructions on the packet. Meanwhile, add 120ml/4fl oz/½ cup of the reserved shellfish liquid to the tomato sauce. Add the basil, prawns, shelled clams and mussels to the sauce. Season.

6 Drain the pasta and tip it into a warmed bowl. Add the sauce and toss well to combine. Serve in individual bowls. Sprinkle with herbs and garnish each portion with lemon, two clams and one mussel in their shells.

Per portion: Energy 510Kcal/2160kJ; Protein 27.2g; Carbohydrate 77.1g, of which sugars 5.6g; Fat 11.5g, of which saturates 1.6g; Cholesterol 68mg; Calcium 180mg; Fibre 3.5g; Sodium 193mg.

SEAFOOD PAELLA

THERE ARE AS MANY VERSIONS OF PAELLA AS THERE ARE REGIONS OF SPAIN. THOSE FROM NEAR THE COAST CONTAIN A LOT OF SEAFOOD, WHILE INLAND VERSIONS ADD CHICKEN OR PORK. HERE THE ONLY MEAT IS THE CHORIZO, ESSENTIAL FOR AN AUTHENTIC FLAVOUR.

SERVES FOUR

INGREDIENTS
45ml/3 tbsp olive oil
1 Spanish (Bermuda) onion, chopped
2 fat garlic cloves, chopped
150g/5oz chorizo sausage, sliced
300g/11oz small squid, cleaned
1 red (bell) pepper, cut into strips
4 tomatoes, peeled, seeded and
  diced, or 200g/7oz can tomatoes
500ml/17fl oz/generous 2 cups
  chicken stock
105ml/7 tbsp dry white wine
200g/7oz/1 cup short grain Spanish
  rice or risotto rice
a large pinch of saffron threads
150g/5oz/1 cup fresh or frozen peas
12 large cooked prawns (shrimp), in
  the shell, or 8 langoustines
450g/1lb fresh mussels, scrubbed
450g/1lb medium clams, scrubbed
salt and ground black pepper

1 Heat the olive oil in a paella pan or wok, add the onion and garlic and cook until translucent. Add the chorizo and cook until lightly golden.

2 If the squid are very small, leave them whole, otherwise cut the bodies into rings and the tentacles into pieces. Add the squid to the pan and sauté over a high heat for 2 minutes.

3 Stir in the pepper strips and tomatoes and simmer gently for 5 minutes, until the pepper strips are tender. Pour in the stock and white wine, stir well and bring to the boil.

4 Stir in the rice and saffron threads and season well with salt and pepper. Spread the contents of the pan evenly. Bring the liquid back to the boil, then lower the heat and simmer gently for about 10 minutes.

5 Add the peas, prawns or langoustines, mussels and clams, stirring them gently into the rice.

6 Cook the paella over a low heat for a further 15–20 minutes, until the rice is tender and all the mussels and clams have opened. If any remain closed, discard them. If the paella seems dry, add a little more hot chicken stock. Gently stir everything together and serve while piping hot.

Per portion: Energy 618Kcal/2600kJ; Protein 41.4g; Carbohydrate 63.8g, of which sugars 10.3g; Fat 21.9g, of which saturates 5.4g; Cholesterol 290mg; Calcium 179mg; Fibre 4.6g; Sodium 1117mg.

OCTOPUS STEW

THIS RUSTIC STEW IS A PERFECT DISH FOR ENTERTAINING, AS IT TASTES EVEN BETTER IF MADE A DAY IN ADVANCE. SERVE WITH A COLOURFUL SALAD OF BABY CHARD, ROCKET AND RADICCHIO.

SERVES FOUR TO SIX

INGREDIENTS
  1kg/2¼lb octopus, cleaned
  45ml/3 tbsp olive oil
  1 large red onion, chopped
  3 garlic cloves, finely chopped
  30ml/2 tbsp brandy
  300ml/½ pint/1¼ cups dry
    white wine
  800g/1¾lb ripe plum tomatoes,
    peeled and chopped, or 2 × 400g/
    14oz cans chopped tomatoes
  1 fresh red chilli, seeded and
    chopped (optional)
  450g/1lb small new potatoes
  15ml/1 tbsp chopped fresh rosemary
  15ml/1 tbsp fresh thyme leaves
  1.2 litres/2 pints/5 cups fish stock
  30ml/2 tbsp fresh flat leaf
    parsley leaves
  salt and ground black pepper
  fresh rosemary sprigs, to garnish
For the garlic croûtes
  1 fat garlic clove, peeled
  8 thick slices of baguette or ciabatta
  30ml/2 tbsp olive oil

3 Pour the brandy over the octopus and ignite it. When the flames have died down, add the wine, bring to the boil and bubble gently for about 5 minutes. Stir in the tomatoes, with the chilli, if using, then add the potatoes, rosemary and thyme. Simmer for 5 minutes.

4 Pour in the fish stock and season well. Cover the pan and simmer for 20–30 minutes, stirring occasionally. The octopus and potatoes should be very tender and the sauce should have thickened slightly. At this stage, you can leave the stew to cool, then put it in the refrigerator overnight.

5 Preheat the grill (broiler). To make the garlic croûtes, cut the garlic clove in half and rub both sides of the slices of baguette or ciabatta with the cut side. Crush the garlic, stir it into the oil and brush the mixture over both sides of the bread. Grill (broil) on both sides until the croûtes are golden brown and crisp.

6 To serve the stew, reheat it gently if it has been in the refrigerator overnight, check the seasoning and stir in the parsley leaves. Serve piping hot in individual warmed bowls, garnished with rosemary sprigs and accompanied by the warm garlic croûtes.

1 Cut the octopus into large pieces, put these in a pan and pour in cold water to cover. Season with salt, bring to the boil, then lower the heat and simmer for 30 minutes to tenderize. Drain and cut into bitesize pieces.

2 Heat the oil in a large shallow pan. Cook the onion for 2–3 minutes, until lightly coloured, then add the garlic and cook for 1 minute more. Add the octopus and cook for 2–3 minutes, stirring to colour it lightly on all sides.

Per portion: Energy 588Kcal/2477kJ; Protein 51.6g; Carbohydrate 41.6g, of which sugars 11.5g; Fat 18.1g, of which saturates 2.8g; Cholesterol 120mg; Calcium 163mg; Fibre 3.8g; Sodium 225mg.

LOUISIANA SEAFOOD GUMBO

GUMBO IS A SOUP, BUT IS SERVED OVER RICE AS A MAIN COURSE. IN LOUISIANA, OYSTERS ARE CHEAP AND PLENTIFUL, AND OYSTERS WOULD BE USED THERE INSTEAD OF MUSSELS.

SERVES SIX

INGREDIENTS
  450g/1lb fresh mussels
  450g/1lb raw prawns (shrimp)
  1 cooked crab, about 1kg/2¼lb
  small bunch of fresh parsley, leaves chopped and stalks reserved
  150ml/¼ pint/⅔ cup vegetable oil
  115g/4oz/1 cup plain (all-purpose) flour
  1 green (bell) pepper, chopped
  1 large onion, chopped
  2 celery sticks, sliced
  3 garlic cloves, finely chopped
  75g/3oz smoked spiced sausage, skinned and sliced
  275g/10oz/1½ cups long grain rice
  6 spring onions (scallions), shredded
  cayenne pepper, to taste
  Tabasco sauce, to taste
  salt

1 Wash the mussels in several changes of cold water, pulling away the black beards. Discard any mussels that are broken or do not close when you tap them firmly.

2 Bring 250ml/8fl oz/1 cup water to the boil in a deep pan. Add the mussels, cover the pan tightly and cook over a high heat, shaking frequently, for 3 minutes. As the mussels open, lift them out with tongs into a sieve set over a bowl. Discard any that fail to open. Shell the mussels, discarding the shells. Return the liquid from the bowl to the pan and make the quantity up to 2 litres/3½ pints/8 cups with water.

3 Peel the prawns and set them aside, reserving a few for the garnish. Put the shells and heads into the pan.

4 Remove all the meat from the crab, separating the brown and white meat. Add all the pieces of shell to the pan with 5ml/2 tsp salt.

5 Bring the shellfish stock to the boil, skimming it regularly. When there is no more froth on the surface, add the parsley stalks and simmer for 15 minutes. Cool, then strain it into a measuring jug (cup) and make up to 2 litres/3½ pints/8 cups with water.

6 Heat the oil in a heavy pan and stir in the flour. Stir constantly over a medium heat with a wooden spoon or whisk until the roux reaches a golden-brown colour. Immediately add the pepper, onion, celery and garlic. Continue cooking for about 3 minutes, until the onion is softened. Stir in the sausage. Reheat the stock.

7 Stir the brown crab meat into the roux, then ladle in the hot stock, a little at a time, stirring constantly until it has all been smoothly incorporated. Bring to a low boil, partially cover the pan, then simmer the gumbo for 30 minutes.

8 Meanwhile, cook the rice in plenty of lightly salted, boiling water until the grains are tender.

9 Add the prawns, mussels, white crab meat and spring onions to the gumbo. Return to the boil and season with salt if necessary, cayenne and a dash or two of Tabasco sauce. Simmer for a further minute, then add the chopped parsley leaves. Serve immediately, ladling the soup over the hot rice in soup plates.

COOK'S TIP
It is essential to stir constantly to darken the roux without burning. Should black specks occur at any stage of cooking, discard the roux and start again. Have the onion, green (bell) pepper and celery ready to add to the roux the minute it reaches the correct golden-brown stage, as this arrests its darkening.

Per portion: Energy 559Kcal/2336kJ; Protein 31.1g; Carbohydrate 57.6g, of which sugars 3.7g; Fat 23g, of which saturates 3.4g; Cholesterol 183mg; Calcium 145mg; Fibre 1.9g; Sodium 474mg.

POULTRY

This chapter includes recipes for all tastes, from grilled skewers, to tagines and croquettes. Try a hearty, traditional Roasted Duckling on a Bed of Honeyed Potatoes, an exotic Thai Stir-fried Chicken with Basil and Chilli, rich and satisfying Caribbean Peanut Chicken, or the ever-popular Tandoori Chicken.

GRILLED SKEWERED CHICKEN

THESE JAPANESE-STYLE KEBABS, SERVED WITH DELICIOUS YAKITORI SAUCE FOR DIPPING, ARE PERFECT FOR EASY ENTERTAINING AND ABSOLUTELY IDEAL FOR A BARBECUE PARTY. FOR AUTHENTICITY, SERVE WITH JAPANESE CONDIMENTS AND SMALL DRINKING BOWLS OF WARM RICE WINE.

SERVES FOUR

INGREDIENTS
   8 chicken thighs with skin, boned
   8 large, thick spring onions
     (scallions), trimmed
For the yakitori sauce
   60ml/4 tbsp sake
   75ml/5 tbsp shoyu
   15ml/1 tbsp mirin
   15ml/1 tbsp caster (superfine) sugar
To serve
   shichimi togarashi, sansho or
     lemon wedges

1 First, make the yakitori sauce. Mix all the ingredients together in a small pan. Bring to the boil, then reduce the heat and simmer for 10 minutes, or until the sauce has thickened.

2 Cut the chicken into 2.5cm/1in cubes with a sharp knife. Cut the spring onions into 2.5cm/1in long sticks.

3 To grill (broil), preheat the grill (broiler) to high. Oil the wire rack and spread out the chicken cubes on it. Grill both sides of the chicken until the juices run, then dip the pieces in the sauce and put back on the rack. Grill for 30 seconds on each side, repeating the dipping process twice more.

4 Set aside and keep warm. Gently grill the spring onions until soft and slightly brown outside. Do not dip. Thread about four pieces of chicken and three spring onion pieces on to each of eight bamboo skewers.

5 Alternatively, to cook on a barbecue, soak eight bamboo skewers overnight in water. This prevents the skewers from burning. Prepare the barbecue. Thread the chicken and spring onion pieces on to skewers, as above. Place the sauce in a small bowl.

6 Cook the skewered chicken on the barbecue. Keep the skewer handles away from the fire, turning them frequently until the juices start to run. Brush the chicken with sauce. Return to the coals and repeat this process twice more until the chicken is well cooked.

7 Arrange the skewers on a platter or individual plates and serve sprinkled with shichimi togarashi or sansho, or accompanied by lemon wedges.

Per portion: Energy 132Kcal/558kJ; Protein 21.6g; Carbohydrate 5.2g, of which sugars 5.1g; Fat 2.9g, of which saturates 0.8g; Cholesterol 105mg; Calcium 18mg; Fibre 0.3g; Sodium 715mg.

GRILLED CHICKEN BALLS COOKED ON BAMBOO SKEWERS

THESE TASTY CHICKEN BALLS, KNOWN AS TSUKUNE, ARE A YAKITORI BAR REGULAR IN JAPAN, AS WELL AS A FAVOURITE FAMILY DISH, AS THEY ARE EASY FOR CHILDREN TO EAT DIRECTLY FROM THE SKEWER. YOU CAN MAKE THE BALLS IN ADVANCE UP TO THE END OF STEP 2, AND THEY FREEZE VERY WELL.

SERVES FOUR

INGREDIENTS
300g/11oz skinless chicken, minced (ground)
2 eggs
2.5ml/½ tsp salt
10ml/2 tsp plain (all-purpose) flour
10ml/2 tsp cornflour (cornstarch)
90ml/6 tbsp dried breadcrumbs
2.5cm/1in piece fresh root ginger, grated
For the "tare" yakitori sauce
60ml/4 tbsp sake
75ml/5 tbsp shoyu
15ml/1 tbsp mirin
15ml/1 tbsp caster (superfine) sugar
2.5ml/½ tsp cornflour (cornstarch) blended with 5ml/1 tsp water
To serve
shichimi togarashi or sansho (optional)

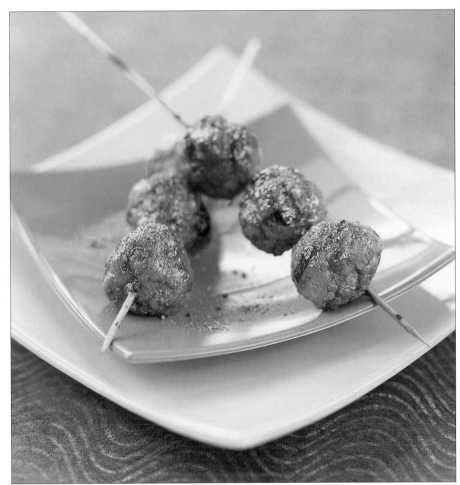

1 Soak eight bamboo skewers overnight in water. Put all the ingredients for the chicken balls, except the ginger, in a food processor and blend well.

2 Wet your hands and scoop about a tablespoonful of the mixture into your palm. Shape it into a small ball about half the size of a golf ball. Make a further 30–32 balls in the same way.

3 Squeeze the juice from the grated ginger into a small mixing bowl. Discard the pulp.

4 Add the ginger juice to a small pan of boiling water. Add the chicken balls, and boil for about 7 minutes, or until the colour of the meat changes and the balls float to the surface. Scoop out using a slotted spoon and drain on a plate covered with kitchen paper.

5 In a small pan, mix all the ingredients for the yakitori sauce, except for the cornflour liquid. Bring to the boil, then reduce the heat and simmer for about 10 minutes, or until the sauce has slightly reduced. Add the cornflour liquid and stir until the sauce is thick. Transfer to a small bowl.

6 Thread three or four balls on to each skewer. Cook under a medium grill (broiler) or on a barbecue, keeping the skewer handles away from the fire. Turn them frequently for a few minutes, or until the balls start to brown. Brush with sauce and return to the heat. Repeat the process twice. Serve, sprinkled with shichimi togarashi or sansho, if you like.

Per portion: Energy 223Kcal/942kJ; Protein 24.2g; Carbohydrate 23.9g, of which sugars 5.1g; Fat 4.1g, of which saturates 1g; Cholesterol 148mg; Calcium 54mg; Fibre 0.6g; Sodium 1031mg.

CHICKEN WITH PEAS

THIS ITALIAN DISH STRONGLY REFLECTS THE TRADITIONS OF BOTH MEDITERRANEAN AND JEWISH COOKING. JEWS FAVOUR THE ENRICHMENT OF MEAT SAUCES WITH EGG BECAUSE OF THE LAWS OF THE KASHRUT, WHICH FORBIDS THE ADDITION OF CREAM TO MEAT DISHES.

SERVES FOUR

INGREDIENTS

4 skinless, boneless chicken
  breast portions
plain (all-purpose) flour, for dusting
30–45ml/2–3 tbsp olive oil
1–2 onions, chopped
¼ fennel bulb, chopped (optional)
15ml/1 tbsp chopped fresh parsley,
  plus extra to garnish
7.5ml/1½ tsp fennel seeds
75ml/5 tbsp dry Marsala
120ml/4fl oz/½ cup chicken stock
300g/11oz/2¼ cups petits pois
  (baby peas)
juice of 1½ lemons
2 egg yolks
salt and ground black pepper

1 Season the chicken with salt and pepper, then dust generously with flour. Shake off the excess flour; set aside.

2 Heat 15ml/1 tbsp oil in a pan, add the onions, fennel, if using, parsley and fennel seeds. Cook for 5 minutes.

3 Add the remaining oil and the chicken to the pan and cook for 2–3 minutes on each side, until lightly browned. Remove the chicken and onion mixture from the pan and set aside.

4 Deglaze the pan by pouring in the Marsala and cooking over a high heat until reduced to about 30ml/2 tbsp, then pour in the stock. Add the peas and return the chicken and onion mixture to the pan. Cook over a very low heat while you prepare the egg mixture.

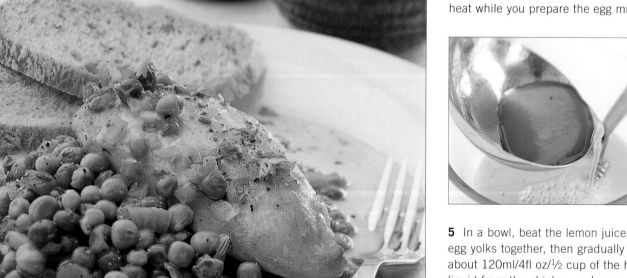

5 In a bowl, beat the lemon juice and egg yolks together, then gradually add about 120ml/4fl oz/½ cup of the hot liquid from the chicken and peas, stirring well to combine.

6 Return the mixture to the pan and cook over a low heat, stirring, until the mixture thickens slightly. (Do not allow the mixture to boil or the eggs will curdle and spoil the sauce.) Serve the chicken immediately, sprinkled with a little extra chopped fresh parsley.

Per portion: Energy 319Kcal/1338kJ; Protein 42g; Carbohydrate 9.1g, of which sugars 5.9g; Fat 10.7g, of which saturates 2.2g; Cholesterol 206mg; Calcium 67mg; Fibre 4.2g; Sodium 150mg.

CHICKEN AND VEGETABLE TAGINE

MOROCCAN TAGINES ARE USUALLY SERVED WITH COUSCOUS, BUT RICE MAKES AN EQUALLY DELICIOUS ACCOMPANIMENT. HERE, COUSCOUS IS STIRRED INTO THE RICE TO CREATE AN UNUSUAL AND TASTY DISH. "TAGINE" IS THE NAME OF THE TRADITIONAL COOKING POT, AS WELL AS THE RECIPE.

SERVES FOUR

INGREDIENTS

 30ml/2 tbsp groundnut (peanut) oil
 4 skinless, boneless chicken breast
   portions, cut into large pieces
 1 large onion, chopped
 2 garlic cloves, crushed
 1 parsnip, cut into 2.5cm/1in pieces
 1 turnip, cut into 2cm/¾in pieces
 3 carrots, cut into 4cm/1½in pieces
 4 tomatoes, chopped
 1 cinnamon stick
 4 cloves
 5ml/1 tsp ground ginger
 1 bay leaf
 1.5–2.5ml/¼–½ tsp cayenne pepper
 350ml/12fl oz/1½ cups chicken stock
 400g/14oz can chickpeas, drained
   and skinned
 1 red (bell) pepper, seeded
   and sliced
 150g/5oz green beans, halved
 1 piece of preserved lemon peel,
   thinly sliced
 20–30 pitted brown or green olives
 salt
For the rice and couscous
 750ml/1¼ pints/3 cups chicken stock
 225g/8oz/generous 1 cup
   long grain rice
 115g/4oz/⅔ cup couscous
 45ml/3 tbsp chopped fresh
   coriander (cilantro)

1 Heat half of the oil in a large pan or flameproof tagine and cook the chicken pieces for a few minutes until evenly browned. Transfer to a plate.

2 Heat the remaining oil and cook the onion, garlic, parsnip, turnip and carrots together over a medium heat for 4–5 minutes until the vegetables are lightly flecked with brown, stirring frequently. Lower the heat, cover and sweat the vegetables for 5 minutes more, stirring occasionally.

3 Add the tomatoes, cook for a few minutes, then add the cinnamon stick, cloves, ginger, bay leaf and cayenne. Cook for 1–2 minutes.

4 Pour in the chicken stock, add the chickpeas and browned chicken pieces, and season with salt. Cover and simmer for 25 minutes.

5 Meanwhile, cook the rice and couscous mixture. Bring the chicken stock to the boil. Add the rice and simmer for about 5 minutes until almost tender. Remove the pan from the heat, stir in the couscous, cover tightly and leave for about 5 minutes.

6 When the vegetables are almost tender, stir in the pepper slices and green beans and simmer for 10 minutes. Add the preserved lemon and olives, stir well and cook for 5 minutes more, or until the vegetables are perfectly tender.

7 Stir the chopped coriander into the rice and couscous mixture and pile it into a warmed serving dish. Transfer the chicken and vegetables into another serving dish, or serve in the tagine.

Per portion: Energy 707Kcal/2985kJ; Protein 52.6g; Carbohydrate 99.5g, of which sugars 16.9g; Fat 13.7g, of which saturates 2.6g; Cholesterol 105mg; Calcium 164mg; Fibre 10.8g; Sodium 344mg.

CHICKEN MARINATED IN MAPLE AND LEMON

THIS IS ONE OF THOSE DISHES THAT MAKES YOU FEEL GOOD ABOUT COOKING FOR FRIENDS. IT IS SIMPLE TO PREPARE, BUT LOOKS AND TASTES AS IF YOU HAVE GONE TO HUGE AMOUNTS OF TROUBLE. SERVE WITH GRILLED VEGETABLES, OR USE SIMPLY DRESSED SALAD LEAVES WITH THE CHICKEN.

SERVES FOUR TO SIX

INGREDIENTS
   4–6 boneless chicken breast
      portions
   115g/4oz firm goat's cheese
   60ml/4 tbsp chopped fresh
      oregano
   20ml/4 tsp maple syrup
   juice of 1 lemon
   oil for brushing
   salt and ground black pepper

COOK'S TIP
You can cook these successfully on a barbecue. Once the flames have died down place a lightly oiled grill rack over the coals to heat. Lay the chicken skin-side up, cover and grill for 15 minutes.

1 Slash a pocket horizontally in each chicken portion. Mix the goat's cheese, chopped oregano and 10ml/2 tsp of the maple syrup in a small bowl. Stuff the pockets in the chicken with the mixture. Don't overfill.

2 Put the remaining maple syrup into a large shallow dish. Stir in the lemon juice and add the chicken portions.

3 Cover and leave in a cool place for 20 minutes, turning occasionally. Season with salt and pepper and marinate for 10 minutes more.

4 Cook the chicken on a hot griddle for about 20 minutes in total. Sear on a high heat, then lower the heat, turning and moving the pieces frequently. Baste with any remaining marinade 5 minutes before the end of cooking.

5 Transfer the chicken to a dish to rest and keep warm for about 5 minutes before serving.

Per portion: Energy 180kcal/756kJ; Protein 28.3g; Carbohydrate 3g, of which sugars 3g; Fat 6.1g, of which saturates 3.7g; Cholesterol 88mg; Calcium 44mg; Fibre 0.3g; Sodium 186mg.

BANG BANG CHICKEN

WHAT A MEMORABLE NAME THIS SPECIAL DISH FROM SICHUAN HAS! USE TOASTED SESAME PASTE TO GIVE THE SAUCE AN AUTHENTIC FLAVOUR, ALTHOUGH CRUNCHY PEANUT BUTTER CAN BE USED INSTEAD. BANG BANG CHICKEN IS PERFECT FOR PARTIES AND IDEAL FOR A BUFFET.

SERVES FOUR

INGREDIENTS
  3 skinless, boneless chicken
    breast portions, total weight
    about 450g/1lb
  1 garlic clove, crushed
  2.5ml/½ tsp black peppercorns
  1 small onion, halved
  1 large cucumber, peeled, seeded
    and cut into thin strips
  salt and ground black pepper
For the sauce
  45ml/3 tbsp toasted sesame paste
  15ml/1 tbsp light soy sauce
  15ml/1 tbsp wine vinegar
  2 spring onions (scallions),
    finely chopped
  2 garlic cloves, crushed
  5 × 1cm/2 × ½in piece fresh
    root ginger, peeled and cut
    into thin batons
  15ml/1 tbsp Sichuan peppercorns,
    dry-fried and crushed
  5ml/1 tsp light brown sugar
For the chilli oil
  60ml/4 tbsp groundnut (peanut) oil
  5ml/1 tsp chilli powder

1 Place the chicken in a large, heavy pan. Pour in sufficient water just to cover, add the garlic, peppercorns and onion and bring to the boil over a medium heat. Skim off any foam that rises to the surface, stir in salt and pepper to taste, then cover the pan. Lower the heat and cook for about 25 minutes, or until the chicken is just tender. Drain, reserving the stock.

2 Make the sauce by mixing the toasted sesame paste with 45ml/3 tbsp of the chicken stock, saving the rest for soup. Add the soy sauce, vinegar, spring onions, garlic, ginger and crushed peppercorns to the sesame mixture. Stir in sugar to taste.

3 Make the chilli oil by gently heating the oil and chilli powder together until foaming. Simmer for 2 minutes, cool, then strain off the red-coloured oil and discard the sediment.

4 Spread out the cucumber batons on a platter. Cut the chicken breast portions into pieces of about the same size as the cucumber strips and arrange them on top. Pour over the sauce, drizzle on the chilli oil and serve.

VARIATION
Crunchy peanut butter can be used instead of sesame paste, if you like. Mix it with 30ml/2 tbsp sesame oil and proceed as in Step 2.

Per portion: Energy 297Kcal/1239kJ; Protein 29.7g; Carbohydrate 2.3g, of which sugars 1.8g; Fat 18.9g, of which saturates 2.6g; Cholesterol 79mg; Calcium 94mg; Fibre 1.4g; Sodium 339mg.

TANDOORI CHICKEN

THE WORD TANDOORI REFERS TO A METHOD OF COOKING IN A CHARCOAL-FIRED CLAY OVEN CALLED A TANDOOR. IN NORTHERN INDIA AND PAKISTAN, A WIDE VARIETY OF FOODS IS COOKED IN THIS TYPE OF OVEN, BUT IN WESTERN COUNTRIES THE METHOD IS MOST POPULAR FOR CHICKEN. WARM NAAN BREAD AND MANGO CHUTNEY MAY BE OFFERED WITH THE CHICKEN AND RICE.

2 Add the cubes of chicken to the casserole and cook for 6 minutes. Stir the water into the tandoori sauce and pour it over the chicken. Bring to the boil, then reduce the heat and simmer for 10 minutes, or until the chicken pieces are cooked through and the sauce is slightly reduced and thickened.

3 Meanwhile, bring a large pan of lightly salted water to the boil, add the turmeric and rice and bring back to the boil. Stir once, reduce the heat to prevent the water from boiling over and simmer the rice for 12 minutes, or according to the time suggested on the packet, until tender.

4 Drain the rice well and serve with the tandoori chicken on warmed individual serving plates, garnished with sprigs of fresh coriander.

SERVES FOUR

INGREDIENTS
30ml/2 tbsp vegetable oil
2 small onions, cut into wedges
2 garlic cloves, sliced
4 skinless, boneless chicken breast portions, cut into cubes
100ml/3½fl oz/⅓ cup water
300g/11oz jar tandoori sauce
salt and ground black pepper
coriander (cilantro) sprigs, to garnish
To serve
5ml/1 tsp ground turmeric
350g/12oz/1⅔ cups basmati rice

1 Heat the oil in a flameproof casserole. Add the onions and garlic, and cook for about 3 minutes, or until the onion is beginning to soften, stirring frequently.

COOK'S TIP
You will find jars of ready-made tandoori sauce in large supermarkets.

Per portion: Energy 592Kcal/2479kJ; Protein 44g; Carbohydrate 77.5g, of which sugars 4.5g; Fat 11.4g, of which saturates 1.1g; Cholesterol 105mg; Calcium 54mg; Fibre 0.4g; Sodium 826mg.

STIR-FRIED CHICKEN WITH BASIL AND CHILLI

THIS QUICK AND EASY CHICKEN DISH IS AN EXCELLENT INTRODUCTION TO THAI CUISINE. THAI BASIL, WHICH IS SOMETIMES KNOWN AS HOLY BASIL, HAS A UNIQUE, PUNGENT FLAVOUR THAT IS BOTH SPICY AND SHARP. DEEP-FRYING THE LEAVES ADDS ANOTHER DIMENSION TO THIS DISH.

SERVES FOUR TO SIX

INGREDIENTS

45ml/3 tbsp vegetable oil
4 garlic cloves, thinly sliced
2–4 fresh red chillies, seeded
  and finely chopped
450g/1lb skinless boneless chicken
  breast portions, diced
45ml/3 tbsp Thai fish sauce
10ml/2 tsp dark soy sauce
5ml/1 tsp sugar
10–12 Thai basil leaves
2 fresh red chillies, seeded and
  finely chopped, and about 20 deep-
  fried Thai basil leaves, to garnish

1 Heat the oil in a wok or large frying pan. Add the garlic and chillies and stir-fry over a medium heat for 1–2 minutes, until the garlic is golden.

2 Add the pieces of chicken to the wok or pan and stir-fry until the chicken changes colour.

3 Stir in the Thai fish sauce, soy sauce and sugar. Continue to stir-fry the mixture for 3–4 minutes, or until the chicken is fully cooked with the sauce.

4 Stir in the fresh Thai basil leaves. Spoon the entire mixture on to a warm serving platter or individual serving dishes, and garnish with the sliced chillies and deep-fried Thai basil.

COOK'S TIP
To deep-fry Thai basil leaves, first make sure that the leaves are completely dry or they will splutter when added to the oil. Deep-fry the leaves briefly in hot oil until they are crisp and translucent – this will take only about 30–40 seconds. Lift out the leaves using a slotted spoon or wire basket and leave them to drain on kitchen paper.

Per portion: Energy 196Kcal/819kJ; Protein 27.2g; Carbohydrate 0.4g, of which sugars 0.4g; Fat 9.5g, of which saturates 1.3g; Cholesterol 79mg; Calcium 7mg; Fibre 0g; Sodium 424mg.

CHICKEN AND PRAWN JAMBALAYA

THE MIXTURE OF CHICKEN, SEAFOOD AND RICE SUGGESTS A CLOSE RELATIONSHIP TO THE SPANISH PAELLA, BUT THE CREOLE NAME IS MORE LIKELY TO HAVE DERIVED FROM JAMBON (THE FRENCH FOR HAM), AND À LA YA (CREOLE FOR RICE). JAMBALAYAS ARE A COLOURFUL MIXTURE OF HIGHLY FLAVOURED INGREDIENTS, AND ARE MADE IN LARGE QUANTITIES FOR FEASTS AND CELEBRATION MEALS.

SERVES TEN

INGREDIENTS

2 chickens, each about 1.5kg/3–3½lb
450g/1lb piece raw smoked gammon
   (cured ham)
50g/2oz/4 tbsp lard or bacon fat
50g/2oz/½ cup plain (all-
   purpose) flour
3 onions, finely sliced
2 green (bell) peppers, seeded
   and sliced
675g/1½lb tomatoes, peeled
   and chopped
2–3 garlic cloves, crushed
10ml/2 tsp chopped fresh thyme
24 large raw prawns (shrimp), peeled
   and deveined
500g/1¼lb/3 cups white long grain rice
2–3 dashes Tabasco sauce
45ml/3 tbsp chopped fresh flat leaf
   parsley, plus sprigs, to garnish
salt and ground black pepper

4 Add the diced gammon, onions, green peppers, tomatoes, garlic and thyme. Cook, stirring regularly, for 10 minutes, then add the prawns and mix lightly.

5 Stir the rice into the pan and pour in 1.2 litres/2 pints/5 cups water. Season to taste with salt, pepper and Tabasco sauce. Bring to the boil over a medium heat, then lower the heat, cover and cook gently until the rice is tender and all the liquid has been absorbed. Add a little extra boiling water if the rice looks as if it might be drying out before it is cooked.

6 Add the chopped flat leaf parsley and gently stir it into the finished dish, garnish with tiny sprigs of flat leaf parsley and serve immediately while piping hot.

1 Cut each chicken into 10 pieces and season with salt and pepper. Dice the gammon, discarding the rind and fat.

2 Melt the lard or bacon fat in a large, heavy frying pan. Add the chicken pieces, in batches, brown them all over, then lift them out with a slotted spoon and set them aside.

3 Reduce the heat. Sprinkle the flour into the fat in the pan and stir until the roux turns golden brown. Return the chicken pieces to the pan.

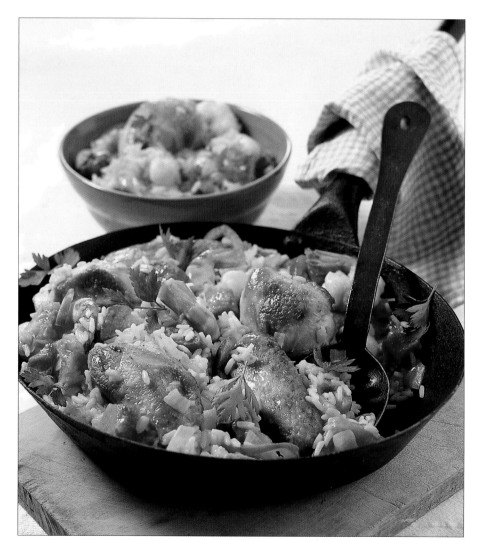

Per portion: Energy 748Kcal/3117kJ; Protein 54.9g; Carbohydrate 50.3g, of which sugars 5.5g; Fat 36.2g, of which saturates 10.8g; Cholesterol 262mg; Calcium 70mg; Fibre 2g; Sodium 588mg.

CARIBBEAN PEANUT CHICKEN

*PEANUT BUTTER IS USED IN MANY CARIBBEAN RECIPES. IT ADDS A RICHNESS TO THE DISHES,
AS WELL AS A DELICIOUS DEPTH OF FLAVOUR ALL OF ITS OWN.*

SERVES FOUR

INGREDIENTS
  4 skinless, boneless chicken breast
    portions, cut into thin strips
  225g/8oz/generous 1 cup white long
    grain rice
  30ml/2 tbsp groundnut (peanut) oil
  15g/½oz/1 tbsp butter, plus extra
    for greasing
  1 onion, finely chopped
  2 tomatoes, peeled, seeded
    and chopped
  1 fresh green chilli, seeded
    and sliced
  60ml/4 tbsp smooth peanut butter
  450ml/¾ pint/scant 2 cups
    chicken stock
  lemon juice, to taste
  salt and ground black pepper
  lime wedges and fresh flat leaf
    parsley sprigs, to garnish
For the marinade
  15ml/1 tbsp sunflower oil
  1–2 garlic cloves, crushed
  5ml/1 tsp chopped fresh thyme
  25ml/1½ tbsp medium curry powder
  juice of half a lemon

1 Mix all the marinade ingredients in a large bowl and stir in the chicken. Cover loosely with clear film (plastic wrap) and set aside in a cool place for 2–3 hours.

2 Meanwhile, cook the rice in plenty of lightly salted, boiling water until tender. Drain well and turn into a generously buttered casserole.

3 Preheat the oven to 180°C/350°F/Gas 4. Heat 15ml/1 tbsp of the oil and butter in a flameproof casserole and cook the chicken pieces for 4–5 minutes, until evenly brown. Add more oil if necessary.

4 Transfer the chicken to a plate. Add the onion to the casserole and cook for 5–6 minutes until lightly browned. Stir in the tomatoes and chilli. Cook over a low heat for 3–4 minutes, stirring occasionally. Remove from the heat.

5 Mix the peanut butter with the chicken stock. Stir into the tomato and onion mixture, then add the chicken. Stir in the lemon juice, season to taste, then spoon the mixture over the rice in the casserole.

6 Cover the casserole, transfer it to the oven and cook for 15–20 minutes, or until piping hot. Use a large spoon to toss the rice with the chicken mixture. Serve immediately, garnished with the lime wedges and parsley sprigs.

COOK'S TIP
If the casserole is not large enough to let you toss the rice with the chicken mixture before serving, invert a large, deep plate over the casserole, turn both over and toss the mixture on the plate.

Per portion: Energy 606Kcal/2532kJ; Protein 46.4g; Carbohydrate 52.6g, of which sugars 5.3g; Fat 23.2g, of which saturates 6.6g; Cholesterol 113mg; Calcium 41mg; Fibre 2.3g; Sodium 202mg.

TURKEY OR CHICKEN SCHNITZEL

IN AUSTRIA, WHERE THIS DISH ORIGINATED, SCHNITZEL WAS ALWAYS MADE FROM VEAL, POUNDED FLAT, CRISPLY COATED AND THEN FRIED. NOWADAYS, IT MAY BE MADE FROM STEAK, CHICKEN OR TURKEY. THIS IS A POPULAR ISRAELI VERSION. SERVE WITH A SELECTION OF VEGETABLES.

SERVES FOUR

INGREDIENTS

4 boneless turkey or chicken breast
   fillets, each weighing about 175g/6oz
juice of 1 lemon
2 garlic cloves, chopped
plain (all-purpose) flour, for dusting
1–2 eggs
15ml/1 tbsp water
about 50g/2oz/½ cup matzo meal
paprika
a mixture of vegetable and olive oil,
   for shallow frying
salt and ground black pepper
lemon wedges and a selection of
   vegetables, to serve (optional)

1 Lay each piece of meat between two sheets of greaseproof (waxed) paper and pound with a mallet or the end of a rolling pin until it is about half its original thickness and fairly even.

2 In a bowl, combine the lemon juice, garlic, salt and pepper. Coat the meat in it, then leave to marinate.

3 Meanwhile, arrange three wide plates or shallow dishes in a row. Fill one plate or dish with flour, beat the egg and water together in another and mix the matzo meal, salt, pepper and paprika together on the third.

4 Working quickly, dip each fillet into the flour, then the egg, then the matzo meal. Pat everything in well, then arrange the crumbed fillets on a plate and chill for at least 30 minutes and up to 2 hours.

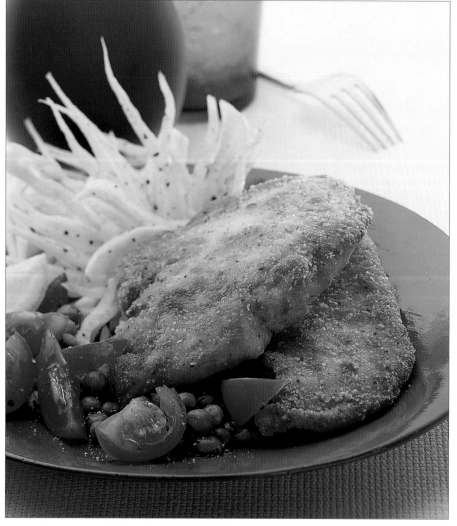

5 In a large, heavy frying pan, heat the oil until it will turn a cube of bread dropped into the oil golden brown in 30–60 seconds. Carefully add the crumbed fillets (in batches if necessary) and cook until golden brown, turning once. Remove and drain on kitchen paper. Serve immediately with lemon wedges and a selection of vegetables.

Per portion: Energy 368Kcal/1546kJ; Protein 45.4g; Carbohydrate 14.7g, of which sugars 0.6g; Fat 14.6g, of which saturates 2.3g; Cholesterol 170mg; Calcium 27mg; Fibre 0.5g; Sodium 125mg.

TURKEY CROQUETTES

*IN THESE CRISP PATTIES, SMOKED TURKEY IS MIXED WITH MASHED POTATO AND SPRING ONIONS,
ROLLED IN BREADCRUMBS, AND SERVED WITH A TANGY TOMATO SAUCE.*

3 Meanwhile, to make the sauce, heat the oil in a frying pan and fry the onion for 5 minutes until softened. Add the tomatoes and purée, stir and simmer for 10 minutes. Stir in the parsley, season with salt and pepper and keep the sauce warm until needed.

SERVES FOUR

INGREDIENTS
  450g/1lb potatoes, diced
  3 eggs
  30ml/2 tbsp milk
  175g/6oz smoked turkey rashers
    (strips), finely chopped
  2 spring onions (scallions),
    thinly sliced
  115g/4oz/2 cups fresh
    white breadcrumbs
  vegetable oil, for deep-frying
For the sauce
  15ml/1 tbsp olive oil
  1 onion, finely chopped
  400g/14oz can tomatoes, drained
  30ml/2 tbsp tomato purée (paste)
  15ml/1 tbsp chopped
    fresh parsley
  salt and ground black pepper

1 Boil the potatoes for 20 minutes, or until tender. Drain and return the pan to a low heat to make sure all the excess water evaporates.

2 Mash the potatoes with two eggs and the milk. Season well with salt and pepper. Stir in the turkey and spring onions. Chill for 1 hour.

4 Remove the potato mixture from the refrigerator and divide into eight pieces. Shape each piece into a sausage shape and dip in the remaining beaten egg and then the breadcrumbs.

5 Heat the vegetable oil in a pan or deep-fryer to 175°C/330°F and deep-fry the croquettes for 5 minutes, or until golden and crisp. Drain and serve immediately with the sauce.

COOK'S TIP
Test the oil is at the correct temperature by dropping a cube of bread on to the surface. If it sinks, rises and sizzles in 10 seconds, the oil is ready to use.

Per portion: Energy 404Kcal/1698kJ; Protein 19.4g; Carbohydrate 47g, of which sugars 7.7g; Fat 16.7g, of which saturates 2.4g; Cholesterol 73mg; Calcium 93mg; Fibre 3.3g; Sodium 315mg.

ROASTED DUCKLING
ON A BED OF HONEYED POTATOES

THE RICH FLAVOUR OF DUCK COMBINED WITH THESE SWEETENED POTATOES GLAZED WITH HONEY MAKES A TRULY LUXURIOUS DISH. SERVE IT WITH STEAMED OR ROASTED VEGETABLES.

SERVES FOUR

INGREDIENTS

 1 duckling, giblets removed
 60ml/4 tbsp light soy sauce
 150ml/¼ pint/⅔ cup fresh
   orange juice
 3 large floury potatoes, cut
   into chunks
 30ml/2 tbsp clear honey
 15ml/1 tbsp sesame seeds
 salt and ground black pepper

1 Preheat the oven to 200°C/400°F/ Gas 6. Place the duckling in a roasting pan. Prick the skin well.

2 Mix the soy sauce and orange juice together and pour over the duck. Cook for 20 minutes.

3 Place the potato chunks in a bowl, stir in the honey and toss to mix well. Remove the duckling from the oven and spoon the potatoes all around and under the duckling.

4 Roast for 35 minutes and remove from the oven. Toss the potatoes in the juices so the underside will be cooked and turn the duck over. Put back in the oven and cook for a further 30 minutes.

5 Remove the duckling from the oven and carefully scoop off the excess fat, leaving the juices behind.

6 Sprinkle the sesame seeds over the potatoes, season and turn the duckling back over, breast side up, and cook for a further 10 minutes. Remove the duckling and potatoes from the oven and keep warm, allowing the duck to stand for a few minutes.

7 Pour off the excess fat and simmer the juices on the hob (stovetop) for a few minutes. Serve the juices with the carved duckling and potatoes.

Per portion: Energy 806Kcal/3341kJ; Protein 20.8g; Carbohydrate 32.3g, of which sugars 6.4g; Fat 66.8g, of which saturates 17.9g; Cholesterol 0mg; Calcium 53mg; Fibre 2.1g; Sodium 403mg.

POT-COOKED DUCK <u>AND</u> GREEN VEGETABLES

PREPARE THE INGREDIENTS FOR THIS JAPANESE DISH BEFOREHAND, SO THAT THE COOKING CAN BE DONE AT THE TABLE. USE A HEAVY PAN OR FLAMEPROOF CASSEROLE WITH A PORTABLE STOVE.

SERVES FOUR

INGREDIENTS
    4 duck breast fillets, about 800g/
        1¾lb total weight
    8 large shiitake mushrooms, stalks
        removed, a cross cut into each cap
    2 leeks, trimmed and cut diagonally
        into 6cm/2½in lengths
    ½ hakusai, stalk part removed and
        cut into 5cm/2in squares
    500g/1¼lb shungiku or mizuna, root
        part removed, cut in half crossways
For the stock
    raw bones from 1 chicken, washed
    1 egg shell
    200g/7oz/scant 1 cup short grain
        rice, washed and drained
    120ml/4fl oz/½ cup sake
    about 10ml/2 tsp coarse sea salt
For the sauce
    75ml/5 tbsp shoyu
    30ml/2 tbsp sake
    juice of 1 lime
    8 white peppercorns, crushed
For the soup
    130g/4½oz Chinese egg noodles,
        cooked and loosened
    1 egg, beaten
    1 bunch of chives
    ground white pepper

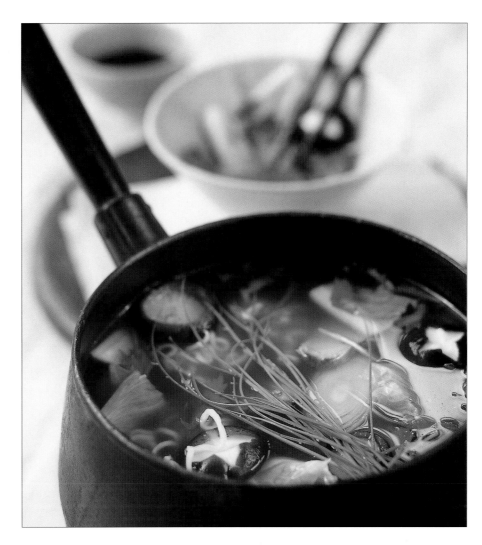

1 To make the stock, put the chicken bones into a pan three-quarters full of water. Bring to the boil and drain when it reaches boiling point. Wash the pan and the bones again, then return to the pan with the same amount of water. Add the egg shell and then bring to the boil. Simmer, uncovered, for 1 hour, skimming frequently. Remove the bones and egg shell. Add the rice, sake and salt, then simmer for 30 minutes. Remove from the heat and set aside.

2 Heat a heavy frying pan until just smoking. Remove from the heat for 1 minute, then add the duck breasts, skin side down. Return to a medium heat and sear for 3–4 minutes, or until crisp. Turn over and sear the other side for 1 minute. Remove from the heat.

3 When cool, wipe the duck fat with kitchen paper and cut the breast and skin into 5mm/¼in thick slices. Arrange on a large serving plate with all the prepared vegetables.

4 Heat through all the ingredients for the sauce in a small pan and transfer to a small jug (pitcher) or bowl.

5 Prepare four dipping bowls, four serving bowls and chopsticks. At the table, bring the pan of soup stock to the boil, then reduce to medium-low. Add half of the shiitake and leeks. Wait for 5 minutes and put in half of the stalk part of the hakusai. Add half of the duck and cook for 1–2 minutes for rare or 5–8 minutes for well-done meat.

6 Each person prepares some duck and vegetables in a serving bowl and drizzles over a little sauce. Add the soft hakusai leaves, shungiku and mizuna to the stock as you eat, adjusting the heat as you go. When the stock is less than a quarter of the pot's volume, top up with 3 parts water to 1 part sake.

7 When the duck has been eaten, bring the reduced stock to the boil. Skim the oil from the surface, and reduce the heat to medium. Add the noodles, cook for 1–2 minutes and check the seasoning. Add more salt if required. Pour in the beaten egg and swirl in the stock. Cover, turn off the heat, then leave to stand for 1 minute. Decorate with the chopped chives and serve with ground pepper.

Per portion: Energy 676Kcal/2846kJ; Protein 53.4g; Carbohydrate 81.6g, of which sugars 9.8g; Fat 19.4g, of which saturates 4.1g; Cholesterol 277mg; Calcium 126mg; Fibre 9.3g; Sodium 1296mg.

MARMALADE-GLAZED GOOSE

SUCCULENT ROAST GOOSE IS THE CLASSIC CENTREPIECE FOR A TRADITIONAL CHRISTMAS LUNCH.
RED CABBAGE COOKED WITH LEEKS, AND BRAISED FENNEL ARE TASTY ACCOMPANIMENTS.

SERVES EIGHT

INGREDIENTS
- 4.5kg/10lb oven-ready goose
- 1 cooking apple, peeled, cored and cut into eighths
- 1 large onion, cut into eighths
- bunch of fresh sage, plus extra sprigs to garnish
- 30ml/2 tbsp ginger marmalade, melted
- salt and ground black pepper

For the stuffing
- 25g/1oz/2 tbsp butter
- 1 onion, finely chopped
- 15ml/1 tbsp ginger marmalade
- 450g/1lb/2 cups ready-to-eat prunes, chopped
- 45ml/3 tbsp Madeira
- 225g/8oz/4 cups fresh white breadcrumbs
- 30ml/2 tbsp chopped fresh sage

For the gravy
- 1 onion, chopped
- 15ml/1 tbsp plain (all-purpose) flour
- 150ml/¼ pint/⅔ cup Madeira
- 600ml/1 pint/2½ cups chicken stock

1 Preheat the oven to 200°C/400°F/ Gas 6. Prick the skin of the goose all over with a fork and season the bird generously, both inside and out.

COOK'S TIP
Red cabbage goes well with goose. Cook 1 small leek, sliced, in 75g/3oz/6 tbsp butter, add 1kg/2¼lb/9 cups shredded red cabbage, with the grated rind of 1 orange, and cook for 2 minutes. Add 30ml/2 tbsp Madeira and 15ml/1 tbsp brown sugar and cook for 15 minutes.

2 Mix the apple, onion and sage leaves and spoon the mixture into the rump end of the goose.

3 To make the stuffing, melt the butter in a large pan and cook the onion for about 5 minutes, or until softened but not coloured. Remove the pan from the heat and stir in the marmalade, chopped prunes, Madeira, breadcrumbs and chopped sage.

4 Stuff the neck end of the goose with some of the stuffing, and set the remaining stuffing aside in the refrigerator. Sew up the bird or secure it with skewers to prevent the stuffing from escaping during cooking.

5 Place the goose in a large roasting pan. Butter a piece of foil and use to cover the goose loosely, then place in the oven for 2 hours.

6 Baste the goose frequently during cooking and remove excess fat from the pan as necessary, using a small ladle or serving spoon. (Strain, cool and chill the fat in a covered container: it is excellent for roasting potatoes.)

7 Remove the foil from the goose and brush the melted ginger marmalade over the goose, then roast for 30–40 minutes more, or until cooked through. To check if the goose is cooked, pierce the thick part of the thigh with a metal skewer; the juices will run clear when the bird is cooked. Remove from the oven and cover with foil, then leave to stand for 15 minutes before carving.

8 While the goose is cooking, shape the remaining stuffing into walnut-size balls and place them in an ovenproof dish. Spoon 30ml/2 tbsp of the goose fat over the stuffing balls and bake for about 15 minutes before the goose is cooked.

9 To make the gravy, pour off all but 15ml/1 tbsp of fat from the roasting pan, leaving the meat juices behind. Add the onion and cook for about 3–5 minutes, or until softened but not coloured. Sprinkle in the flour and then gradually stir in the Madeira and stock. Bring to the boil, stirring constantly, then simmer for 3 minutes, or until thickened and glossy. Strain the gravy and serve it with the carved goose and stuffing. Garnish with sage leaves.

Per portion: Energy 823Kcal/3443kJ; Protein 57.6g; Carbohydrate 47.1g, of which sugars 23.8g; Fat 43.3g, of which saturates 14g; Cholesterol 177mg; Calcium 106mg; Fibre 4.5g; Sodium 395mg.

MEAT AND GAME

Meat-loving dinner guests are sure to be impressed by any of the dishes in this chapter, whether you choose a traditional Roast Pork with Sage and Onion Stuffing or Rich Game Pie, fragrant Beef Biryani or mildly curried Spiced Lamb with Tomatoes and Peppers. Cantonese Fried Noodles, otherwise known as Chow Mein, is always popular, and Beef Enchiladas with Red Sauce will definitely please lovers of hot chilli.

  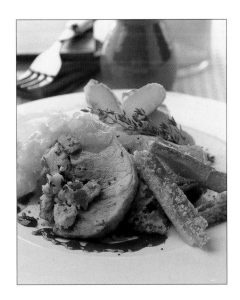

STUFFED BUTTERFLY OF BEEF WITH CHEESE AND CHILLI SAUCE

THIS RECIPE HAD ITS ORIGINS IN NORTHERN MEXICO OR IN NEW MEXICO, WHICH IS BEEF COUNTRY. IT IS A GOOD WAY TO COOK STEAKS, EITHER UNDER THE GRILL OR ON THE BARBECUE.

SERVES FOUR

INGREDIENTS
    4 fresh serrano chillies
    115g/4oz/½ cup full-fat soft cheese
    30ml/2 tbsp reposada tequila
    30ml/2 tbsp oil
    1 onion
    2 garlic cloves
    5ml/1 tsp dried oregano
    2.5ml/½ tsp salt
    2.5ml/½ tsp ground black pepper
    175g/6oz/1½ cups grated medium
      Cheddar cheese
    4 fillet steaks, at least 2.5cm/
      1in thick

1 Dry-roast the chillies in a griddle pan over a medium heat, turning them frequently until the skins are blistered but not burnt. Put them in a strong plastic bag and tie the top to keep the steam in. Set aside for 20 minutes.

2 Remove the chillies from the bag, slit them and scrape out the seeds with a sharp knife. Cut the flesh into long narrow strips, then cut each strip into several shorter strips.

3 Put the full-fat soft cheese in a small heavy pan and stir over a very low heat until it has melted. Add the chilli strips and the tequila and stir to make a smooth sauce. Keep warm over a very low heat.

4 Heat the oil in a frying pan and cook the onion, garlic and oregano for about 5 minutes over a moderate heat, stirring frequently until the onion has browned. Season with the salt and pepper.

5 Remove the pan from the heat and add the grated Cheddar cheese, in two or three batches. Stir well so that it melts into the onion and garlic mixture without becoming rubbery.

6 Cut each steak almost but not quite in half across its width, so that it can be opened out, butterfly-fashion. Preheat the grill (broiler) to its highest setting.

7 Spoon a quarter of the cheese and onion filling on to one side of each steak and close the other side over it. Place the steaks in a grill pan and grill (broil) for 3–5 minutes on each side, depending on how you like your steak. Serve on heated plates with the vegetables of your choice, and with the cheese and chilli sauce poured over.

COOK'S TIP
One of the easiest ways of testing whether a steak is cooked is by touch. A steak that is very rare or "blue" will feel soft to the touch; the meat will be relaxed. A rare steak will feel like a sponge, and will spring back when lightly pressed. A medium-rare steak offers more resistance, while a well-cooked steak will feel very firm.

Per portion: Energy 580Kcal/2412kJ; Protein 51.1g; Carbohydrate 3g, of which sugars 2.2g; Fat 39.5g, of which saturates 20.6g; Cholesterol 175mg; Calcium 372mg; Fibre 0.5g; Sodium 735mg.

STEAK BÉARNAISE

BÉARNAISE, AFTER BÉARN IN SOUTH-WEST FRANCE, IS A CREAMY EGG AND BUTTER SAUCE FLAVOURED WITH FRESH TARRAGON. IT IS A CLASSIC COMPLEMENT TO GRIDDLED, GRILLED OR PAN-FRIED STEAK AND ALSO EXCELLENT WITH ROAST BEEF. ROASTED VEGETABLES MAKE A GOOD ACCOMPANIMENT.

SERVES FOUR

INGREDIENTS
    4 sirloin steaks, each weighing about
      225g/8oz, trimmed
    15ml/1 tbsp sunflower oil (optional)
    salt and ground black pepper
For the Béarnaise sauce
    90ml/6 tbsp white wine vinegar
    12 black peppercorns
    2 bay leaves
    2 shallots, finely chopped
    4 fresh tarragon sprigs
    4 egg yolks
    225g/8oz/1 cup unsalted (sweet)
      butter at room temperature, diced
    30ml/2 tbsp chopped fresh tarragon
    ground white pepper

1 Start by making the sauce. Put the vinegar, peppercorns, bay leaves, shallots and tarragon sprigs in a small pan and simmer until reduced to 30ml/2 tbsp. Strain the vinegar through a fine sieve.

2 Beat the egg yolks with salt and freshly ground white pepper in a small, heatproof bowl. Stand the bowl over a pan of very gently simmering water, then gradually beat the strained vinegar into the yolks.

3 Gradually beat in the butter, one piece at a time, allowing each addition to melt before adding the next. Do not allow the water to heat beyond a gentle simmer or the sauce will overheat and curdle.

4 While cooking the sauce, heat a griddle or grill until very hot.

COOK'S TIP
If you are confident about preparing egg and butter sauces, the best method is to reduce the flavoured vinegar before cooking the steak, then finish the sauce while the steak is cooking. This way, the sauce does not have to be kept hot and there is less risk of overheating it or allowing it to become too thick.

5 Beat the chopped fresh tarragon into the sauce and remove the pan from the heat. The sauce should be smooth, thick and glossy.

6 Cover the surface of the sauce with clear film (plastic wrap) or dampened greaseproof (waxed) paper to prevent a skin forming and leave over the pan of hot water, still off the heat, to keep hot while you cook the steak.

7 Season the steaks with salt and plenty freshly ground black pepper.

8 A pan is not usually oiled before cooking steak, but if it is essential to grease the pan, add only the minimum oil. Cook the steaks for 2–4 minutes on each side. The cooking time depends on the thickness of the steaks and the extent to which you want to cook them. As a guide, 2–4 minutes will give a medium-rare result.

9 Serve the steaks on warmed plates. Peel the clear film or dampened greaseproof paper off the sauce and stir it lightly, then spoon it over the steaks.

Per portion: Energy 796Kcal/3297kJ; Protein 51.1g; Carbohydrate 0.5g, of which sugars 0.4g; Fat 65.5g, of which saturates 37.2g; Cholesterol 459mg; Calcium 50mg; Fibre 0.2g; Sodium 450mg.

THAI CRISPY NOODLES WITH BEEF

RICE VERMICELLI ARE VERY FINE, DRY, WHITE NOODLES BUNDLED IN LARGE FRAGILE LOOPS AND SOLD IN PACKETS. THEY ARE DEEP-FRIED BEFORE BEING ADDED TO THIS DISH, AND IN THE PROCESS THEY EXPAND TO AT LEAST FOUR TIMES THEIR ORIGINAL SIZE.

SERVES FOUR

INGREDIENTS

about 450g/1lb rump (round) or
  sirloin steak
teriyaki sauce, for sprinkling
175g/6oz rice vermicelli
groundnut (peanut) oil for deep-frying
  and stir-frying
8 spring onions (scallions),
  diagonally sliced
2 garlic cloves, crushed
4–5 carrots, cut into julienne strips
1–2 fresh red chillies, seeded and
  finely sliced
2 small courgettes (zucchini),
  diagonally sliced
5ml/1 tsp grated fresh root ginger
60ml/4 tbsp white or yellow
  rice vinegar
90ml/6 tbsp light soy sauce
about 475ml/16fl oz/2 cups
  spicy stock

1 Using a meat mallet or the side of a rolling pin, beat out the steak, if necessary, to about 2.5cm/1in thick. Place in a shallow dish, brush generously with the teriyaki sauce and set aside for 2–4 hours to marinate.

2 Separate the rice vermicelli into manageable loops and spread several layers of kitchen paper on a very large plate. Pour the oil into a large wok to a depth of about 5cm/2in, and heat until a strand of vermicelli cooks as soon as it is lowered into the oil.

3 Carefully add a loop of rice vermicelli to the oil. It should immediately expand and become opaque. Turn the noodles over so that the strands cook on both sides and then transfer the cooked noodles to the prepared plate to drain. Repeat the process until all the noodles have been cooked. Transfer the cooked rice vermicelli to a separate wok or a deep serving bowl and keep them warm while you are cooking the steak and vegetables.

4 Strain the oil from the wok into a heatproof bowl and set it aside. Heat 15ml/1 tbsp groundnut oil in the clean wok. When it sizzles, cook the steak for about 30 seconds on each side until browned. Transfer to a board and cut into thick slices. The meat should be well browned on the outside but still pink inside. Set aside.

5 Add a little extra oil to the wok and stir-fry the spring onions, garlic and carrots over a medium heat for about 5–6 minutes until the carrots are slightly soft and glazed. Add the chillies, courgettes and ginger and stir-fry for 1–2 minutes more.

6 Stir in the rice vinegar, soy sauce and stock. Cook for about 4 minutes, until the sauce has slightly thickened. Add the steak and cook for a further 1–2 minutes (or longer, if you prefer your meat well done).

7 Pour the steak, vegetables and all the mixture over the noodles and toss lightly and carefully to mix, then serve.

COOK'S TIP
As soon as you add the meat mixture to the noodles, they will soften. If you wish to keep a few crispy noodles, stir some to the surface so they do not come into contact with the hot liquid.

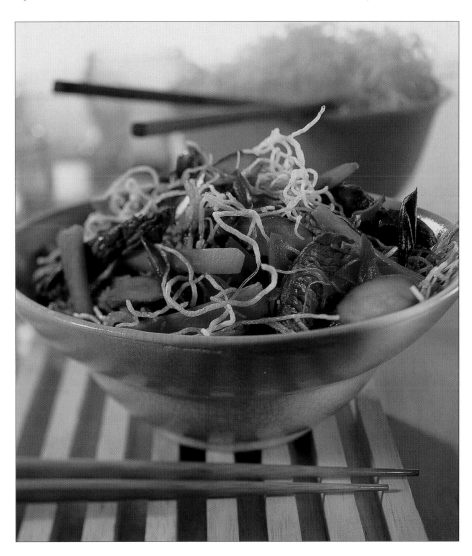

Per portion: Energy 510Kcal/2122kJ; Protein 30.7g; Carbohydrate 41.6g, of which sugars 6.8g; Fat 24.5g, of which saturates 5.7g; Cholesterol 66mg; Calcium 51mg; Fibre 2.1g; Sodium 1262mg.

BEEF CARBONADE

THIS RICH, DARK STEW OF BEEF, COOKED SLOWLY WITH LOTS OF ONIONS, GARLIC AND BEER, IS A CLASSIC CASSEROLE FROM THE NORTH OF FRANCE AND NEIGHBOURING BELGIUM.

3 Reduce the heat and return the onions to the pan. Add the garlic, cook briefly, then add the beer or ale, water and sugar. Tie the thyme and bay leaf together and add to the pan with the celery. Bring to the boil, stirring, then season with salt and pepper.

4 Pour the sauce over the beef and mix well. Cover tightly, then place in the oven for 2½ hours. Check the beef once or twice to make sure that it is not too dry, adding a little water, if necessary. Test for tenderness, allowing an extra 30–40 minutes' cooking if necessary.

SERVES SIX

INGREDIENTS
    45ml/3 tbsp vegetable oil or
      beef dripping (drippings)
    3 onions, sliced
    45ml/3 tbsp plain (all-purpose) flour
    2.5ml/½ tsp mustard powder
    1kg/2¼lb boneless beef shin (shank)
      or chuck, cut into large cubes
    2–3 garlic cloves, finely chopped
    300ml/½ pint/1¼ cups dark beer or ale
    150ml/¼ pint/⅔ cup water
    5ml/1 tsp dark brown sugar
    1 fresh thyme sprig
    1 fresh bay leaf
    1 piece celery stick
    salt and ground black pepper
For the topping
    50g/2oz/¼ cup butter
    1 garlic clove, crushed
    15ml/1 tbsp Dijon mustard
    45ml/3 tbsp chopped fresh parsley
    6–12 slices baguette or ficelle loaf

1 Preheat the oven to 160°C/325°F/Gas 3. Heat 30ml/2 tbsp of the oil or dripping in a frying pan and cook the onions over a low heat until softened. Remove from the pan and set aside.

2 Meanwhile, mix together the flour and mustard and season. Toss the beef in the flour. Add the remaining oil or dripping to the pan and heat over a high heat. Brown the beef all over, then transfer it to a casserole.

5 To make the topping, cream the butter with the garlic, mustard and 30ml/2 tbsp of the parsley. Spread the butter thickly over the bread. Increase the oven temperature to 190°C/375°F/Gas 5. Taste and season the casserole, then arrange the bread slices, buttered side uppermost, on top. Bake for 20–25 minutes, until the bread is browned and crisp. Sprinkle the remaining parsley over the top and serve immediately.

Per portion: Energy 577Kcal/2410kJ; Protein 42.8g; Carbohydrate 32.8g, of which sugars 9.6g; Fat 28.8g, of which saturates 11.5g; Cholesterol 114mg; Calcium 87mg; Fibre 2.1g; Sodium 414mg.

BEEF ENCHILADAS <u>WITH</u> RED SAUCE

ENCHILADAS ARE USUALLY MADE WITH CORN TORTILLAS, ALTHOUGH IN PARTS OF NORTHERN MEXICO WHEAT FLOUR TORTILLAS ARE SOMETIMES USED.

SERVES THREE TO FOUR

INGREDIENTS

500g/1¼lb rump (round) steak, cut into 5cm/2in cubes
2 ancho chillies, seeded
2 pasilla chillies, seeded
2 garlic cloves, crushed
10ml/2 tsp dried oregano
2.5ml/½ tsp ground cumin
30ml/2 tbsp vegetable oil
7 fresh corn tortillas
shredded onion and flat leaf parsley, to garnish
mango salsa, to serve

1 Put the steak in a deep frying pan and cover with water. Bring to the boil, then lower the heat and simmer for 1–1½ hours, or until very tender.

2 Meanwhile, put the dried chillies in a bowl and pour over the hot water. Leave to soak for 30 minutes, then tip the contents of the bowl into a blender and process to a smooth paste.

3 Drain the steak and let it cool, reserving 250ml/8fl oz/1 cup of the cooking liquid. Meanwhile, cook the garlic, oregano and cumin in the oil for 2 minutes.

4 Stir in the chilli paste and the reserved cooking liquid from the steak. Tear one of the tortillas into small pieces and add it to the mixture. Bring to the boil, then lower the heat. Simmer for 10 minutes, stirring occasionally, until thickened. Shred the steak, using two forks, stir it into the sauce and heat through for a few minutes.

5 Spoon some of the meat mixture on to each tortilla and roll it up to make an enchilada. Keep the enchiladas in a warmed dish until you have rolled them all. Garnish with shreds of onion and fresh flat leaf parsley and then serve immediately with the mango salsa.

VARIATION
For a richer version place the rolled enchiladas side by side in a gratin dish. Pour over 300ml/½ pint/1¼ cups sour cream and 75g/3oz/¾ cup grated Cheddar cheese. Place under a preheated grill (broiler) for 5 minutes, or until the cheese melts and the sauce begins to bubble. Serve with the salsa.

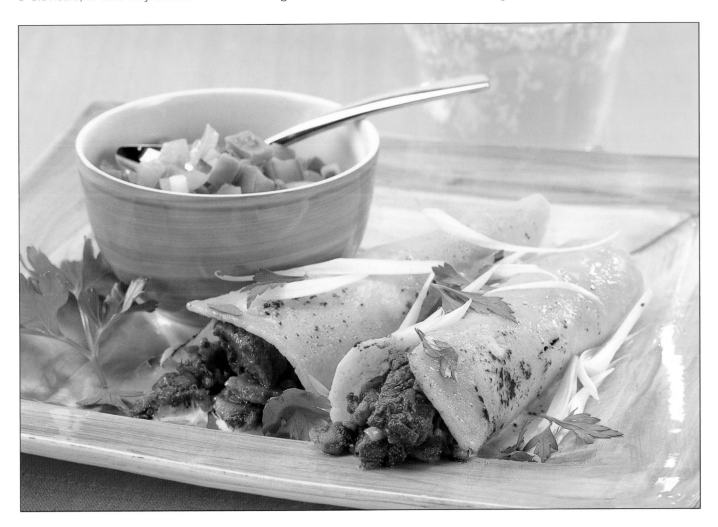

Per portion: Energy 477Kcal/2004kJ; Protein 40.6g; Carbohydrate 39.9g, of which sugars 0.9g; Fat 18.3g, of which saturates 5.5g; Cholesterol 102mg; Calcium 85mg; Fibre 1.6g; Sodium 261mg.

BEEF BIRYANI

THE MOGULS INTRODUCED THIS DRY, SPICY RICE DISH TO CENTRAL INDIA.

SERVES FOUR

INGREDIENTS

2 large onions
2 garlic cloves, chopped
2.5cm/1in piece of fresh root ginger, peeled and coarsely chopped
½–1 fresh green chilli, seeded and coarsely chopped
bunch of fresh coriander (cilantro)
60ml/4 tbsp flaked (sliced) almonds
30–45ml/2–3 tbsp water
15ml/1 tbsp ghee or butter, plus 25g/1oz/2 tbsp butter, for the rice
45ml/3 tbsp sunflower oil
30ml/2 tbsp sultanas (golden raisins)
500g/1¼lb braising or stewing steak, cubed
5ml/1 tsp ground coriander
15ml/1 tbsp ground cumin
2.5ml/½ tsp ground turmeric
2.5ml/½ tsp ground fenugreek
good pinch of ground cinnamon
175ml/6fl oz/¾ cup natural (plain) yogurt
275g/10oz/1½ cups basmati rice
about 1.2 litres/2 pints/5 cups hot chicken stock or water
salt and ground black pepper
2 hard-boiled eggs, quartered, to garnish

1 Coarsely chop 1 onion and place it in a food processor or blender. Add the garlic, ginger, chilli, fresh coriander and half the flaked almonds. Pour in the water and process to a smooth paste.

2 Thinly slice the remaining onion into rings or half rings. Heat half the ghee or butter with half the oil in a heavy, flameproof casserole and cook the onion rings over a medium heat for 10–15 minutes, until they are a deep golden brown. Transfer to a plate with a slotted spoon. Cook the remaining flaked almonds briefly until golden and set aside with the onion rings, then quickly cook the sultanas until they swell. Transfer to the plate.

3 Heat the remaining ghee or butter in the casserole with a further 15ml/1 tbsp of the oil. Cook the meat, in batches, until evenly browned. Transfer to a plate and set aside.

4 Wipe the casserole clean with kitchen paper, heat the remaining oil and pour in the onion and ginger paste. Cook over a medium heat, stirring constantly, for 2–3 minutes, until the mixture begins to brown lightly. Stir in the ground coriander, cumin, turmeric, fenugreek and cinnamon, season to taste with salt and pepper and cook for 1 minute more.

5 Lower the heat, then gradually stir in the yogurt, a little at a time. When all of it has been incorporated into the spice mixture, return the meat to the casserole. Stir to coat, cover tightly and simmer over a gentle heat for about 40–45 minutes, until the meat is tender.

6 Meanwhile, place the rice in a large bowl, pour in cold water to cover and leave to soak for 15–20 minutes.

7 Preheat the oven to 160°C/325°F/ Gas 3. Drain the rice, place it in a pan and add the hot chicken stock or water, together with a little salt. Bring back to the boil, cover, lower the heat and cook for 5–6 minutes.

8 Drain the rice and pile it in a mound on top of the meat in the casserole. Using the handle of a spoon, make a hole through the rice and meat mixture, to the base of the pan. Sprinkle the onion rings, almonds and sultanas over the top and dot with butter. Cover the casserole tightly with a double layer of foil and secure with a lid.

9 Cook the biryani in the oven for 30–40 minutes. To serve, spoon the mixture on to a warmed serving plate and garnish with the quartered hard-boiled eggs. Serve with parathas, naan bread or chapatis, if you like.

COOK'S TIP

When you are cooking the onion and ginger paste and the ground spices, reduce the heat to very low and stir constantly to avoid scorching them.

Per portion: Energy 778Kcal/3240kJ; Protein 40g; Carbohydrate 70.4g, of which sugars 13.4g; Fat 37.4g, of which saturates 11.8g; Cholesterol 94mg; Calcium 164mg; Fibre 2.3g; Sodium 183mg.

PAN-FRIED CALF'S LIVER
WITH CRISP ONIONS

SAUTÉED OR CREAMY MASHED POTATOES GO WELL WITH FRIED CALF'S LIVER. SERVE A SALAD OF MIXED LEAVES WITH PLENTY OF DELICATE FRESH HERBS, SUCH AS FENNEL, DILL AND PARSLEY, TO COMPLEMENT THE SIMPLE FLAVOURS OF THIS MAIN COURSE.

SERVES FOUR

INGREDIENTS
  50g/2oz/¼ cup butter
  4 onions, thinly sliced
  5ml/1 tsp caster (superfine) sugar
  4 slices calf's liver, each weighing
    about 115g/4oz
  30ml/2 tbsp plain (all-purpose) flour
  30ml/2 tbsp olive oil
  salt and ground black pepper
  parsley, to garnish

1 Melt the butter in a large, heavy pan with a lid. Add the onions and mix well to coat with butter. Cover the pan with a tight-fitting lid and cook gently for 10 minutes, stirring occasionally.

2 Stir in the sugar and cover the pan. Cook the onions for 10 minutes more, or until they are soft and golden. Increase the heat, remove the lid and stir the onions over a high heat until they are deep gold and crisp. Use a slotted spoon to remove the onions from the pan, draining off the fat.

3 Meanwhile, rinse the calf's liver in cold water and pat it dry on kitchen paper. Season the flour, put it on a plate and turn the slices of liver in it until they are lightly coated in flour.

COOK'S TIP
Take care not to cook the liver for too long as this may cause it to toughen.

4 Heat the oil in a large frying pan, add the liver and cook for about 2 minutes on each side, or until lightly browned and just firm. Arrange the liver on warmed plates, with the crisp onions. Garnish with parsley and serve with sautéed or mashed potatoes.

KOFTA KEBABS

THESE SPICY PATTIES OF MINCED LAMB ARE SPIKED WITH AROMATIC HERBS AND SEASONINGS. THEY ARE VERY POPULAR THROUGHOUT THE MIDDLE EAST RIGHT THROUGH TO THE INDIAN SUBCONTINENT. SERVE WITH FLAT BREAD AND A SELECTION OF REFRESHING AND EXOTIC SALADS, SUCH AS ORANGES SPRINKLED WITH CAYENNE OR PAPRIKA, ONIONS SPRINKLED WITH SUMAC, AND TOMATO WEDGES WITH HERBS AND CHILLIES.

SERVES FOUR

INGREDIENTS

  450g/1lb minced (ground) lamb
  1–2 large slices of French bread,
    very finely crumbled
  ½ bunch fresh coriander (cilantro),
    finely chopped
  5 garlic cloves, chopped
  1 onion, finely chopped
  juice of ½ lemon
  5ml/1 tsp ground cumin
  5ml/1 tsp paprika
  15ml/1 tbsp curry powder
  pinch each of ground cardamom,
    turmeric and cinnamon
  15ml/1 tbsp tomato purée (paste)
  cayenne pepper or chopped fresh
    chillies (optional)
  1 egg, beaten, if needed
  salt and ground black pepper
  flat bread and salads, to serve

1 Put the lamb, crumbled bread, coriander, garlic, onion, lemon juice, spices, tomato purée, cayenne pepper or chillies and seasoning in a large bowl. Mix well. If the mixture does not bind together, add the beaten egg and a little more bread.

2 With wet hands, shape the mixture into four large or eight small patties.

3 Heat a heavy, non-stick frying pan, add the patties and cook, taking care that they do not fall apart, and turning once or twice, until browned. Serve hot with flat bread and salads.

VARIATION
Mix a handful of raisins or sultanas (golden raisins) into the meat mixture before shaping it into patties.

Per portion: Energy 414Kcal/1740kJ; Protein 29.3g; Carbohydrate 36.9g, of which sugars 4.1g; Fat 17.7g, of which saturates 7.6g; Cholesterol 134mg; Calcium 131mg; Fibre 2.5g; Sodium 470mg.

SPICED LAMB WITH TOMATOES AND PEPPERS

SELECT LEAN TENDER LAMB FROM THE LEG FOR THIS LIGHTLY SPICED CURRY WITH SUCCULENT PEPPERS AND ONION WEDGES. SERVE WITH WARM NAAN BREAD TO MOP UP THE TOMATO-RICH JUICES.

SERVES SIX

INGREDIENTS
1.5kg/3¼lb boneless lamb, cubed
250ml/8fl oz/1 cup natural
  (plain) yogurt
30ml/2 tbsp sunflower oil
3 onions
2 red (bell) peppers, seeded and cut
  into chunks
3 garlic cloves, finely chopped
1 red chilli, seeded and chopped
2.5cm/1in piece fresh root ginger,
  peeled and chopped
30ml/2 tbsp mild curry paste
2 x 400g/14oz cans tomatoes
large pinch of saffron threads
800g/1¾lb plum tomatoes, halved,
  seeded and cut into chunks
salt and ground black pepper
chopped fresh coriander (cilantro),
  to garnish

1 Mix the lamb with the yogurt in a bowl. Cover and chill for about 1 hour. (Marinating in yogurt helps to tenderize the meat and reduce the cooking time.)

2 Heat the oil in a karahi, wok or large pan. Drain the lamb and reserve the yogurt, then cook the lamb, in batches, until it is golden on all sides – this takes about 15 minutes in total. Remove from the pan and set aside.

3 Cut two of the onions into wedges (six from each onion) and add to the oil remaining in the pan. Cook the onion wedges over a medium heat for about 10 minutes, or until they are beginning to colour. Add the peppers and cook for a further 5 minutes. Use a slotted spoon to remove the vegetables from the pan and set aside.

4 Meanwhile, chop the remaining onion. Add it to the oil remaining in the pan with the garlic, chilli and ginger, and cook, stirring frequently, until softened.

5 Stir in the curry paste and canned tomatoes with the reserved yogurt marinade. Replace the lamb, add seasoning to taste and stir well. Bring to the boil, reduce the heat and simmer for about 30 minutes.

6 Pound the saffron to a powder in a mortar, then stir in a little boiling water to dissolve it. Add this liquid to the curry. Replace the onion and pepper mixture. Stir in the fresh tomatoes and bring back to simmering point, then cook for 15 minutes. Garnish with chopped coriander to serve.

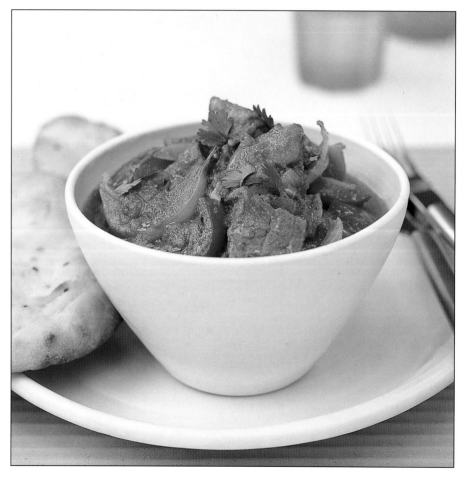

Per portion: Energy 587Kcal/2456kJ; Protein 54.7g; Carbohydrate 19.5g, of which sugars 17.7g; Fat 33g, of which saturates 13.8g; Cholesterol 191mg; Calcium 143mg; Fibre 4g; Sodium 318mg.

LAMB POT-ROASTED <u>WITH</u> TOMATOES, BEANS <u>AND</u> ONIONS

THIS SLOW-BRAISED DISH OF LAMB AND TOMATOES, SPICED WITH CINNAMON AND STEWED WITH GREEN BEANS, SHOWS A GREEK INFLUENCE. IT IS ALSO GOOD MADE WITH COURGETTES INSTEAD OF BEANS.

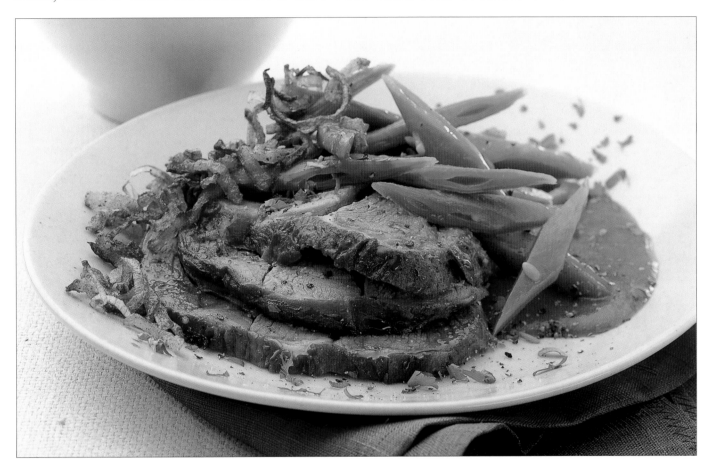

SERVES EIGHT

INGREDIENTS

1kg/2¼ lb lamb on the bone
8 garlic cloves, chopped
2.5–5ml/½–1 tsp ground cumin
45ml/3 tbsp olive oil
juice of 1 lemon
2 onions, thinly sliced
about 500ml/17fl oz/2¼ cups
  lamb, beef or vegetable stock
75–90ml/5–6 tbsp tomato
  purée (paste)
1 cinnamon stick
2–3 large pinches of ground
  allspice or ground cloves
15–30ml/1–2 tbsp sugar
400g/14oz/scant 3 cups
  green beans
salt and ground black pepper
15–30ml/1–2 tbsp chopped
  fresh parsley, to garnish

1 Preheat the oven to 160°C/325°F/Gas 3. Coat the lamb with the garlic, cumin, olive oil, lemon juice, salt and pepper.

2 Heat a flameproof casserole. Sear the lamb on all sides. Add the onions and pour the stock over the meat to cover. Stir in the tomato purée, spices and sugar. Cover and cook in the oven for 2–3 hours.

3 Remove the casserole from the oven and pour the stock into a pan. Move the onions to the side of the dish and return to the oven, uncovered, for 20 minutes.

4 Meanwhile, add the beans to the hot stock and cook until the beans are tender and the sauce has thickened. Slice the meat and serve with the pan juices and beans. Garnish with parsley.

Per portion: Energy 333Kcal/1394kJ; Protein 39.1g; Carbohydrate 8.2g, of which sugars 6.9g; Fat 16.2g, of which saturates 5.4g; Cholesterol 125mg; Calcium 41mg; Fibre 2g; Sodium 109mg.

LAMB'S LIVER AND BACON CASSEROLE

BOILED NEW POTATOES TOSSED IN LOTS OF BUTTER GO WELL WITH THIS SIMPLE CASSEROLE. THE TRICK WHEN COOKING LIVER IS TO SEAL IT QUICKLY, THEN SIMMER IT GENTLY AND BRIEFLY. PROLONGED AND/OR FIERCE COOKING MAKES LIVER HARD AND GRAINY.

SERVES FOUR

INGREDIENTS
    30ml/2 tbsp sunflower oil
    225g/8oz rindless unsmoked back
      (lean) bacon rashers (strips), cut
      into pieces
    2 onions, halved and sliced
    175g/6oz/2⅓ cups chestnut
      mushrooms, halved
    450g/1lb lamb's liver, trimmed
      and sliced
    25g/1oz/2 tbsp butter
    15ml/1 tbsp soy sauce
    30ml/2 tbsp plain (all-purpose) flour
    150ml/¼ pint/⅔ cup chicken stock
    salt and ground black pepper

1 Heat the oil in a frying pan and cook the bacon until crisp. Add the onions to the pan and cook for about 10 minutes, stirring frequently, or until softened. Add the mushrooms to the pan and cook for a further 1 minute.

2 Use a slotted spoon to remove the bacon and vegetables from the pan and set aside. Add the liver to the pan and cook over a high heat for 3–4 minutes, turning once to seal the slices on both sides. Remove the liver from the pan and keep warm.

3 Melt the butter in the pan, add the soy sauce and flour and blend together. Stir in the stock and bring to the boil, stirring until thickened. Return the liver and vegetables to the pan and heat through for 1 minute. Season with salt and pepper to taste, and serve with new potatoes and lightly cooked green beans.

Per portion: Energy 434Kcal/1809kJ; Protein 34.7g; Carbohydrate 13g, of which sugars 3.9g; Fat 27.4g, of which saturates 9.4g; Cholesterol 527mg; Calcium 43mg; Fibre 1.6g; Sodium 1258mg.

SPANISH PORK AND SAUSAGE CASSEROLE

THIS DISH IS FROM THE CATALAN REGION OF SPAIN, AND COMBINES PORK CHOPS WITH SPICY BUTIFARRA SAUSAGES IN A RICH TOMATO SAUCE. YOU CAN FIND THESE SAUSAGES IN SOME SPANISH DELICATESSENS BUT, IF NOT, SWEET ITALIAN SAUSAGES WILL DO.

SERVES FOUR

INGREDIENTS

- 30ml/2 tbsp olive oil
- 4 boneless pork chops, about 175g/6oz each
- 4 butifarra or sweet Italian sausages
- 1 onion, chopped
- 2 garlic cloves, chopped
- 120ml/4fl oz/½ cup dry white wine
- 6 plum tomatoes, chopped
- 1 bay leaf
- 30ml/2 tbsp chopped fresh parsley
- salt and ground black pepper
- baked potatoes and green salad, to serve

1 Heat the oil in a large, deep frying pan. Cook the pork chops over a high heat until browned on both sides, then transfer to a plate.

2 Add the sausages, onion and garlic to the pan and cook over a medium heat until the sausages are browned and the onion softened, turning the sausages two or three times during cooking. Return the chops to the pan.

3 Stir in the wine, tomatoes, bay leaf and parsley. Season. Cover the pan and cook for 30 minutes.

4 Remove the sausages and cut into thick slices. Return them to the pan and heat through. Serve with baked potatoes and a green salad.

Per portion: Energy 431Kcal/1803kJ; Protein 44.3g; Carbohydrate 12.5g, of which sugars 6.9g; Fat 20.8g, of which saturates 6.5g; Cholesterol 127mg; Calcium 78mg; Fibre 2.4g; Sodium 618mg.

PORK ESCALOPES BAKED <u>WITH</u> APPLE <u>AND</u> POTATO RÖSTI

THE JUICES FROM THE PORK COOK INTO THE APPLES AND POTATOES GIVING THEM A WONDERFUL FLAVOUR AS WELL AS MAKING A DELICIOUS SAUCE.

SERVES FOUR

INGREDIENTS
2 large potatoes, finely grated
1 medium cooking apple, grated
2 garlic cloves, crushed
1 egg, beaten
butter, for greasing
15ml/1 tbsp olive oil
4 large prosciutto slices
4 pork escalopes (US scallops), about
175g/6oz each
4 sage leaves
1 medium cooking apple,
cut into thin wedges
25g/1oz/2 tbsp butter, diced
salt and ground black pepper
caramelized apple wedges, to serve

COOK'S TIPS
• Take care not to overcook the pork as it will start to dry out.
• If you can't find cooking apples, use an all-purpose eating variety, such as Granny Smith.

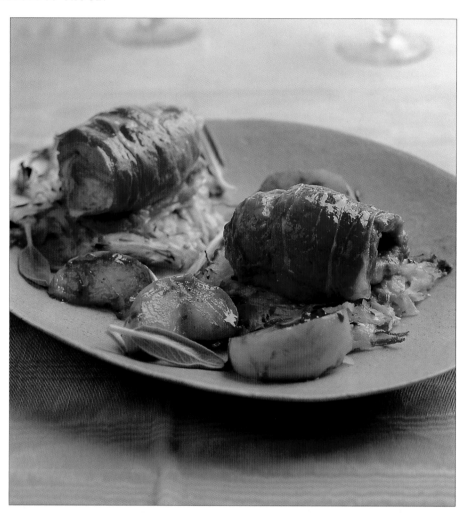

1 Preheat the oven to 200°C/400°F/ Gas 6. Squeeze out all the excess liquid from the grated potatoes and apple. Mix the grated ingredients together with the garlic, egg and seasoning.

2 Divide the potatoes into four portions and spoon each quarter on to a baking sheet that has been lined with foil and greased. Form a round with the potatoes and flatten out slightly with the back of a spoon. Drizzle with a little olive oil. Cook for 10 minutes.

3 Meanwhile, lay the prosciutto on a clean surface and place a pork escalope on top. Lay a sage leaf and apple wedges over each escalope and top each piece with the butter. Wrap the prosciutto around each piece of meat, making sure it is covered completely.

4 Remove the potatoes from the oven, place each pork parcel on top and return to the oven for 20 minutes. Carefully lift the pork and potatoes off the foil and serve with caramelized wedges of apple and any cooking juices on the side.

Per portion: Energy 396Kcal/1659kJ; Protein 42.7g; Carbohydrate 19.2g, of which sugars 4.4g; Fat 16.9g, of which saturates 6.7g; Cholesterol 177mg; Calcium 29mg; Fibre 1.5g; Sodium 310mg.

ROAST PORK WITH SAGE AND ONION STUFFING

SAGE AND ONION MAKE A CLASSIC STUFFING FOR ROAST PORK, DUCK AND TURKEY, WITH THE SAGE COUNTERACTING THE FATTINESS OF THE RICH MEATS. SERVE WITH APPLE SAUCE AND ROAST POTATOES.

SERVES SIX TO EIGHT

INGREDIENTS
1.3–1.6kg/3–3½lb boneless loin of pork
60ml/4 tbsp fine, dry breadcrumbs
10ml/2 tsp chopped fresh sage
25ml/1½ tbsp plain (all-
   purpose) flour
300ml/½ pint/1¼ cups (hard) cider
150ml/¼ pint/⅔ cup water
5–10ml/1–2 tsp crab apple or
   redcurrant jelly
salt and ground black pepper
fresh thyme sprigs, to garnish
For the stuffing
25g/1oz/2 tbsp butter
50g/2oz bacon, finely chopped
2 large onions, finely chopped
75g/3oz/1½ cups fresh
   white breadcrumbs
30ml/2 tbsp chopped fresh sage
5ml/1 tsp chopped fresh thyme
10ml/2 tsp finely grated lemon rind
1 small (US medium)
   egg, beaten

1 Preheat the oven to 220°C/425°F/ Gas 7. To make the stuffing, melt the butter in a pan and cook the bacon until it begins to brown, then add the onions and cook gently until softened. Mix with the breadcrumbs, sage, thyme, lemon rind and egg, then season well.

2 Cut the rind off the piece of pork in one piece and score it well. Cooking the rind separately makes crisper crackling than leaving it on the pork.

3 Place the pork fat side down, and season. Add a layer of stuffing, then roll up and tie neatly.

4 Lay the rind over the pork and rub in 5ml/1 tsp salt. Roast for 2–2½ hours, basting with the pork fat once or twice. Reduce the temperature to 190°C/375°F/ Gas 5 after 20 minutes. Shape the remaining stuffing into balls and add to the roasting pan for the last 30 minutes.

5 Remove the rind from the pork. Increase the oven temperature to 220°C/425°F/Gas 7 and roast the rind for a further 20–25 minutes, until crisp.

6 Mix the dry breadcrumbs and sage and press them into the fat. Cook the pork for 10 minutes, then cover and set aside in a warm place for 15–20 minutes.

7 Remove all but 30–45ml/2–3 tbsp of the fat from the roasting pan and place it on the hob (stovetop). Stir in the flour, followed by the cider and water. Bring to the boil and then cook gently for 10 minutes. Strain the gravy into a clean pan, add the crab apple or redcurrant jelly, and cook for another 5 minutes. Adjust the seasoning.

8 Serve the pork cut into thick slices and the crisp crackling cut into strips with the cider gravy, garnished with thyme.

Per portion: Energy 426Kcal/1789kJ; Protein 52.4g; Carbohydrate 23.7g, of which sugars 5.3g; Fat 14.1g, of which saturates 5.7g; Cholesterol 180mg; Calcium 67mg; Fibre 1.4g; Sodium 475mg.

CANTONESE FRIED NOODLES

CHOW MEIN *IS HUGELY POPULAR WITH THE THRIFTY CHINESE WHO BELIEVE IN TURNING LEFTOVERS INTO TASTY DISHES. FOR THIS DELICIOUS DISH, BOILED NOODLES ARE FRIED TO FORM A CRISPY CRUST, WHICH IS TOPPED WITH A SAVOURY SAUCE CONTAINING WHATEVER TASTES GOOD AND NEEDS EATING UP.*

2 Heat a third of the oil in a large wok or frying pan and sauté the noodles. After turning them over once, press the noodles evenly against the base of the pan with a wooden spatula until they form a flat, even cake. Cook over a medium heat for about 4 minutes, or until the noodles on the underside have become crisp.

3 Turn the noodle cake over with a spatula or fish slice or invert on to a large plate and slide back into the wok. Cook for 3 minutes more, then slide on to a heated plate. Keep warm.

4 Heat 30ml/2 tbsp of the remaining oil in the wok. Add the strips of leek, then the meat strips and stir-fry for 10–15 seconds. Sprinkle over half the soy sauce and then add the bamboo shoots and mushrooms, with salt and pepper to taste. Toss over the heat for 1 minute, then transfer this mixture to a plate and set aside.

SERVES TWO TO THREE

INGREDIENTS
225g/8oz lean beef steak or pork
   fillet (tenderloin)
225g/8oz can bamboo shoots, drained
1 leek, trimmed
25g/1oz Chinese dried mushrooms,
   soaked for 30 minutes in 120ml/
   4fl oz/½ cup warm water
150g/5oz Chinese leaves
   (Chinese cabbage)
450g/1lb cooked egg noodles
   (255g/8oz dried), drained well
90ml/6 tbsp vegetable oil
30ml/2 tbsp dark soy sauce
15ml/1 tbsp cornflour (cornstarch)
15ml/1 tbsp rice wine or dry sherry
5ml/1 tsp sesame oil
5ml/1 tsp caster (superfine) sugar
salt and ground black pepper

1 Slice the beef or pork, bamboo shoots and leek into thin batons. Drain the mushrooms, reserving 90ml/6 tbsp of the soaking water. Cut off and discard the stems, then slice the caps finely. Cut the Chinese leaves into 2.5cm/1in diamond-shaped pieces and sprinkle with salt. Pat the noodles dry with kitchen paper.

5 Heat the remaining oil in the wok and sauté the Chinese leaves for 1 minute. Return the meat and vegetable mixture to the wok and sauté with the leaves for 30 seconds, stirring constantly.

6 Mix the cornflour with the reserved mushroom water. Stir into the wok along with the rice wine or sherry, sesame oil, sugar and remaining soy sauce. Cook for 15 seconds to thicken. Divide the noodles among serving dishes and pile the meat and vegetables on top.

Per portion: Energy 695Kcal/2895kJ; Protein 35.3g; Carbohydrate 38.8g, of which sugars 7.7g; Fat 45.3g, of which saturates 8.5g; Cholesterol 79mg; Calcium 79mg; Fibre 4.6g; Sodium 1185mg.

FIVE-FLAVOUR NOODLES

THE JAPANESE NAME FOR THIS DISH IS GOMOKU YAKISOBA, MEANING FIVE DIFFERENT INGREDIENTS; HOWEVER, YOU CAN ADD AS MANY DIFFERENT INGREDIENTS AS YOU WISH TO MAKE AN EXCITING AND TASTY NOODLE STIR-FRY.

SERVES FOUR

INGREDIENTS
   300g/11oz dried Chinese thin egg
      noodles or 500g/1¼lb fresh yaki-
      soba noodles
   200g/7oz lean boneless pork,
      thinly sliced
   22.5ml/4½ tsp sunflower oil
   10g/¼oz grated fresh root ginger
   1 garlic clove, crushed
   200g/7oz green cabbage,
      coarsely chopped
   115g/4oz/2 cups beansprouts
   1 green (bell) pepper, seeded and cut
      into fine strips
   1 red (bell) pepper, seeded and cut
      into fine strips
   salt and ground black pepper
   20ml/4 tsp ao-nori seaweed, to
      garnish (optional)

For the seasoning mix
   60ml/4 tbsp Worcestershire sauce
   15ml/1 tbsp Japanese soy sauce
   15ml/1 tbsp oyster sauce
   15ml/1 tbsp sugar
   2.5ml/½ tsp salt
   ground white pepper

1 Cook the noodles according to the instructions on the packet. Drain well and set aside.

2 Cut the pork into 3–4cm/1¼–1½in strips and season with salt and pepper.

3 Heat 7.5ml/1½ tsp of the oil in a large wok or frying pan. Add the pork and stir-fry until it is just cooked, then remove it from the pan.

4 Wipe the wok with kitchen paper, and heat the remaining oil in it. Add the ginger, garlic and cabbage and stir-fry for 1 minute.

5 Add the beansprouts, stir until softened, then add the green and red peppers and stir-fry for 1 minute more.

6 Return the pork to the pan and add the noodles. Stir in all the ingredients for the seasoning mix and stir-fry for 2–3 minutes. Serve immediately, sprinkled with ao-nori seaweed, if using.

Per portion: Energy 437Kcal/1848kJ; Protein 22.7g; Carbohydrate 65.6g, of which sugars 12.4g; Fat 11.2g, of which saturates 2.8g; Cholesterol 54mg; Calcium 64mg; Fibre 5.1g; Sodium 686mg.

ROAST VEAL WITH PARSLEY STUFFING

COOKING THIS LOIN OF VEAL, WITH ITS FRAGRANT PARSLEY AND LEEK STUFFING, IN A ROASTING BAG MAKES SURE THAT IT IS SUCCULENT AND FULL-FLAVOURED WHEN SERVED.

SERVES SIX

INGREDIENTS
  25g/1oz/2 tbsp butter
  15ml/1 tbsp sunflower oil
  1 leek, finely chopped
  1 celery stick, finely chopped
  50g/2oz/1 cup fresh
    white breadcrumbs
  50g/2oz/½ cup chopped fresh flat
    leaf parsley
  900g/2lb boned loin of veal
  salt and ground black pepper

VARIATION
Other mild herbs can be used in the stuffing instead of parsley. Try tarragon, chervil and chives, but avoid strong-flavoured herbs, such as marjoram, oregano and thyme, which tend to overpower the delicate flavour of veal.

1 Preheat the oven to 180°C/350°F/Gas 4. Heat the butter and oil in a frying pan until foaming. Cook the leek and celery until they are just starting to colour, then remove the pan from the heat and stir in the breadcrumbs, parsley and seasoning.

2 Lay the loin of veal out flat. Spread the stuffing over the meat, then roll it up carefully and tie the roll at regular intervals to secure it in a neat shape.

3 Place the veal in a roasting bag and close the bag with an ovenproof tie, then place it in a roasting pan. Roast the veal for 1¼ hours.

4 Pierce the meat with a metal skewer to check whether it is cooked: when cooked the meat juices will run clear. Leave the veal to stand for about 10–15 minutes, then carve it into thick slices and serve with gravy, sautéed potatoes, asparagus and sugar snaps.

ESCALOPES OF VEAL WITH CREAM SAUCE

THIS QUICK, EASY DINNER-PARTY DISH IS DELICIOUS SERVED WITH BUTTERED TAGLIATELLE AND LIGHTLY STEAMED GREEN VEGETABLES.

SERVES FOUR

INGREDIENTS
  15ml/1 tbsp plain (all-purpose) flour
  4 veal escalopes (US scallops), each
    weighing about 75–115g/3–4oz
  30ml/2 tbsp sunflower oil
  1 shallot, chopped
  150g/5oz/2 cups oyster
    mushrooms, sliced
  30ml/2 tbsp Marsala or
    medium-dry sherry
  200ml/7fl oz/scant 1 cup
    crème fraîche
  30ml/2 tbsp chopped fresh tarragon
  salt and ground black pepper

COOK'S TIP
If the sauce seems to be too thick, add 30ml/2 tbsp water.

1 Season the flour and use to dust the veal escalopes, then set aside.

2 Heat the oil in a large frying pan and cook the shallot and mushrooms for 5 minutes. Add the escalopes and cook over a high heat for about 1½ minutes on each side. Pour in the Marsala or sherry and cook until reduced by half.

3 Use a spatula to remove the veal escalopes from the pan. Stir the crème fraîche, tarragon and seasoning into the juices remaining in the pan and simmer gently for 3–5 minutes, or until the sauce is thick and creamy.

4 Return the escalopes to the pan and heat through for 1 minute before serving.

Top per portion: Energy 233Kcal/981kJ; Protein 33.4g; Carbohydrate 7.6g, of which sugars 1.1g; Fat 7.9g, of which saturates 3.6g; Cholesterol 135mg; Calcium 49mg; Fibre 1.3g; Sodium 260mg.
Below per portion: Energy 376Kcal/1564kJ; Protein 25g; Carbohydrate 5.5g, of which sugars 1.5g; Fat 27.5g, of which saturates 14.9g; Cholesterol 108mg; Calcium 44mg; Fibre 0.6g; Sodium 73mg.

RICH GAME PIE

TERRIFIC FOR STYLISH PICNICS OR JUST AS SMART FOR A FORMAL WEDDING BUFFET, THIS PIE LOOKS SPECTACULAR WHEN BAKED IN A FLUTED RAISED PIE MOULD. SOME SPECIALIST KITCHEN STORES HIRE THE MOULDS SO THAT YOU CAN AVOID THE EXPENSE OF PURCHASING THEM; ALTERNATIVELY A 20CM/8IN ROUND SPRINGFORM TIN CAN BE USED.

SERVES TEN

INGREDIENTS
  25g/1oz/2 tbsp butter
  1 onion, finely chopped
  2 garlic cloves, finely chopped
  900g/2lb mixed boneless game
    meat, such as skinless pheasant
    and/or pigeon (US squab) breast,
    venison and rabbit, diced
  30ml/2 tbsp chopped mixed fresh
    herbs such as parsley, thyme
    and marjoram
  salt and ground black pepper
For the pâté
  50g/2oz/¼ cup butter
  2 garlic cloves, finely chopped
  450g/1lb chicken livers, rinsed,
    trimmed and chopped
  60ml/4 tbsp brandy
  5ml/1 tsp ground mace
For the hot water crust pastry
  675g/1½lb/6 cups strong white
    bread flour
  5ml/1 tsp salt
  115ml/3½fl oz/scant ½ cup milk
  115ml/3½fl oz/scant ½ cup water
  115g/4oz/½ cup lard, diced
  115g/4oz/½ cup butter, diced
  beaten egg, to glaze
For the jelly
  300ml/½ pint/1¼ cups game or
    beef consommé
  2.5ml/½ tsp powdered gelatine

1 Melt the butter in a small pan, then add the onion and garlic and cook until softened but not coloured. Remove from the heat and mix with the diced game meat and the chopped mixed herbs. Season well, cover and chill.

2 To make the pâté, melt the butter in a pan until foaming. Add the garlic and chicken livers and cook until the livers are just browned. Remove the pan from the heat and stir in the brandy and mace. Process the mixture in a blender or food processor to a smooth purée, then set aside and leave to cool.

3 To make the pastry, sift the flour and salt into a bowl and make a well in the centre. Place the milk and water in a pan. Add the lard and butter and heat gently until melted, then bring to the boil and remove from the heat as soon as the mixture begins to bubble. Pour the hot liquid into the well in the flour and beat until smooth. Cover and leave until cool enough to handle.

4 Preheat the oven to 200°C/400°F/ Gas 6. Roll out two-thirds of the pastry and use to line a 23cm/9in raised pie mould. Spoon in half the game mixture and press it down evenly. Add the pâté and then top with the remaining game.

5 Roll out the remaining pastry to form a lid. Brush the edge of the pastry lining the mould with a little water and cover the pie with the pastry lid. Trim off excess pastry from around the edge. Pinch the edges together to seal in the filling. Make two holes in the centre of the lid and glaze with egg. Use pastry trimmings to roll out leaves to garnish the pie. Brush with egg.

6 Bake the pie for 20 minutes, then cover it with foil and cook for a further 10 minutes. Reduce the oven temperature to 150°C/300°F/Gas 2. Glaze the pie again with beaten egg and cook for a further 1½ hours, keeping the top covered loosely with foil.

7 Remove the pie from the oven and leave it to stand for 15 minutes. Increase the oven temperature to 200°C/400°F/Gas 6. Stand the mould on a baking sheet and remove the sides. Quickly glaze the sides of the pie with beaten egg and cover the top with foil, then cook for a final 15 minutes to brown the sides. Leave to cool completely, then chill the pie overnight.

8 To make the jelly, heat the game or beef consommé in a small pan until just beginning to bubble, whisk in the gelatine until dissolved and leave to cool until just setting. Using a small funnel, carefully pour the jellied consommé into the holes in the pie. Chill until set. This pie will keep in the refrigerator for up to 3 days.

Per portion: Energy 731Kcal/3058kJ; Protein 44g; Carbohydrate 54.3g, of which sugars 2.5g; Fat 32g, of which saturates 17.9g; Cholesterol 223mg; Calcium 163mg; Fibre 2.3g; Sodium 444mg.

VEGETARIAN

This chapter provides a wide range of delicious and satisfying main courses that will delight any vegetarian dinner guest. You could opt for a variation on a dish normally made with meat, such as the succulent Roasted Ratatouille Moussaka, or one of the many traditional vegetarian dishes, including spicy Indian Mee Goreng, Risotto with Four Cheeses, and Classic Cheese Soufflé.

LEEK ROULADE WITH CHEESE, WALNUT AND SWEET PEPPER FILLING

THIS ROULADE IS SURPRISINGLY EASY TO PREPARE, AND IT MAKES A GOOD MAIN COURSE WHEN SERVED WITH HOME-MADE TOMATO SAUCE. IT IS ALSO EXCELLENT AS PART OF A BUFFET.

SERVES FOUR TO SIX

INGREDIENTS

 butter or oil, for greasing
 30ml/2 tbsp fine dry
  white breadcrumbs
 75g/3oz/1 cup finely grated
  Parmesan cheese
 50g/2oz/¼ cup butter
 2 leeks, thinly sliced
 40g/1½oz/⅓ cup plain (all-
  purpose) flour
 250ml/8fl oz/1 cup milk
 5ml/1 tsp Dijon mustard
 1.5ml/¼ tsp freshly grated nutmeg
 2 large (US extra large) eggs,
  separated, plus 1 egg white
 2.5ml/½ tsp cream of tartar
 salt and ground black pepper
 rocket (arugula) and balsamic
  dressing, to serve
For the filling
 2 large red (bell) peppers
 350g/12oz/1½ cups ricotta cheese,
 90g/3½oz/scant 1 cup
  chopped walnuts
 4 spring onions (scallions), chopped
 15g/½oz/½ cup fresh basil leaves

1 Grease and line a 30 × 23cm/
12 × 9in Swiss roll tin (jelly roll pan) with
baking parchment, then sprinkle with
the breadcrumbs and 30ml/2 tbsp
of the grated Parmesan. Preheat the
oven to 190°C/375°F/Gas 5.

2 Melt the butter in a pan and cook the
leeks for 5 minutes, until softened.

3 Stir in the flour and cook over a low
heat, stirring constantly, for 2 minutes,
then gradually stir in the milk. Cook for
3–4 minutes, stirring constantly to make
a thick sauce.

4 Stir in the mustard and nutmeg and
season with salt and plenty of pepper.
Reserve 30–45ml/2–3 tbsp of the
remaining Parmesan, then stir the rest
into the sauce. Cool slightly.

5 Beat the egg yolks into the sauce. In
a scrupulously clean bowl, whisk the
egg whites and cream of tartar until
stiff. Stir 2–3 spoonfuls of the egg white
into the leek mixture, then carefully fold
in the remaining egg white.

6 Pour the mixture into the tin and
gently level it out using a spatula. Bake
for 15–18 minutes, until risen and just
firm to a light touch in the centre. If the
roulade is to be served hot, increase the
oven temperature to 200°C/400°F/Gas 6
after removing the roulade.

7 Meanwhile, heat the grill (broiler).
Halve and seed the peppers, then grill
(broil) them, skin sides uppermost, until
black. Place in a bowl, cover and leave
for 10 minutes. Peel and cut into strips.

8 Beat the cheese with the walnuts and
spring onions. Chop half the basil and
beat it into the mixture. Season to taste.

9 Place a large sheet of baking
parchment on the work surface and
sprinkle with the remaining Parmesan.
Turn out the roulade on to it. Strip off
the lining paper and allow the roulade
to cool slightly. Spread the cheese
mixture over it and top with the red
pepper strips. Tear the remaining basil
leaves and sprinkle them over the top.

10 Using the parchment as a guide, roll
up the roulade and roll it on to a serving
platter. If serving hot, roll the roulade on
to a baking sheet, cover with a tent of
foil and bake for 15–20 minutes. Serve
with rocket and drizzle with dressing.

Per portion: Energy 602Kcal/2500kJ; Protein 32.9g; Carbohydrate 22.3g, of which sugars 13.7g; Fat 44.1g, of which saturates 18g; Cholesterol 184mg; Calcium 486mg; Fibre 4.3g; Sodium 740mg.

CLASSIC CHEESE SOUFFLÉ

A LIGHT, DELICATE, MELT-IN-THE-MOUTH CHEESE SOUFFLÉ MAKES ONE OF THE MOST DELIGHTFUL BRUNCHES IMAGINABLE. ALL YOU NEED TO GO WITH IT IS SALAD, A GLASS OF GOOD WINE AND PLENTY OF TIME TO RELAX AND ENJOY A LAZY WEEKEND.

SERVES TWO TO THREE

INGREDIENTS
  50g/2oz/¼ cup butter
  30–45ml/2–3 tbsp dried breadcrumbs
  200ml/7fl oz/scant 1 cup milk
  30g/1¼oz/3 tbsp plain (all-
    purpose) flour
  pinch of cayenne pepper
  2.5ml/½ tsp mustard powder
  50g/2oz/½ cup mature (sharp) grated
    Cheddar cheese
  25g/1oz/⅓ cup freshly grated
    Parmesan cheese
  4 eggs, separated, plus 1 egg white
  salt and ground black pepper

2 Heat the milk in a large pan. Add the remaining butter, flour and cayenne, with the mustard powder. Bring to the boil over a low heat, whisking steadily until the mixture thickens to a smooth sauce.

5 Add a few spoonfuls of the beaten egg whites to the sauce to lighten it. Beat well, then tip the rest of the whites into the pan and, with a large metal spoon, gently fold in the egg whites, using a figure-of-eight movement to combine the mixtures.

1 Preheat the oven to 190°C/375°F/ Gas 5. Melt 15ml/1 tbsp of the butter and use to grease a 1.2 litre/2 pint/ 5 cup soufflé dish thoroughly. Coat the inside of the dish with breadcrumbs. Shake out any excess.

3 Simmer the sauce for a minute or two, then turn off the heat and whisk in all the Cheddar and half the Parmesan. Cool a little, then beat in the egg yolks. Check the seasoning; the mixture should be well seasoned. Set aside.

6 Pour the mixture into the prepared soufflé dish, level the top and, to help the soufflé rise evenly, run your finger around the inside rim of the dish.

7 Place the dish on a baking sheet. Sprinkle the remaining Parmesan over the top of the soufflé mixture and bake for about 25 minutes, until risen and golden brown. Serve immediately.

VARIATIONS
• Crumbled blue cheese, such as Stilton, Shropshire Blue or Fourme d'Ambert, will produce a soufflé with a much stronger, sharper flavour.
• This soufflé can also be served as a more substantial main meal by adding a few extra ingredients. Try putting a layer of chopped vegetables, such as ratatouille or sautéed mushrooms, at the base of the dish before adding the cheese mixture. Bake as above.

4 Whisk the egg whites in a large grease-free bowl until they form soft, glossy peaks. Do not overbeat or the whites will become grainy and difficult to fold in.

COOK'S TIP
It is important to serve soufflé the moment it is cooked and taken from the oven. Otherwise, the wonderful puffed top may sink before it reaches the expectantly waiting diners.

Per portion: Energy 654Kcal/2721kJ; Protein 31.9g; Carbohydrate 28.2g, of which sugars 5.5g; Fat 46.1g, of which saturates 25.3g; Cholesterol 476mg; Calcium 558mg; Fibre 0.8g; Sodium 797mg.

ROASTED SQUASH

Gem squash has a sweet, subtle flavour that contrasts well with olives and sun-dried tomatoes in this recipe. The rice adds substance without changing any of the flavours.

2 Mix the rice, tomatoes, olives, cheese, half the olive oil and basil in a bowl.

3 Oil a shallow ovenproof dish with the remaining oil, just large enough to hold the squash side by side. Divide the rice mixture among the squash and place them in the dish.

SERVES FOUR

INGREDIENTS

  4 whole gem squashes
  225g/8oz/2 cups cooked white
    long grain rice
  75g/3oz/1½ cups sun-dried
    tomatoes in oil, drained
    and chopped
  50g/2oz/½ cup pitted black
    olives, chopped
  60ml/4 tbsp soft goat's cheese
  30ml/2 tbsp olive oil
  15ml/1 tbsp chopped fresh basil
    leaves, plus fresh basil sprigs,
    to serve
  yogurt and mint dressing
    or green salad,
    to serve (optional)

1 Preheat the oven to 180°C/350°F/ Gas 4. Using a sharp knife, trim away the base of each gem squash and then slice off the tops. Using a spoon, scoop out and discard the seeds.

4 Cover with foil and bake for about 45–50 minutes, until the squash is tender when pierced with the point of a sharp knife or skewer. Garnish with basil sprigs and serve with a yogurt and mint dressing or with a green salad if you like.

Per portion: Energy 280Kcal/1170kJ; Protein 8.7g; Carbohydrate 23.6g, of which sugars 5g; Fat 17.4g, of which saturates 6.3g; Cholesterol 23mg; Calcium 125mg; Fibre 3.1g; Sodium 434mg.

POTATO GNOCCHI <u>WITH</u> SIMPLE TOMATO <u>AND</u> BUTTER SAUCE

GNOCCHI MAKE A SUBSTANTIAL AND TASTY ALTERNATIVE TO PASTA. IN THIS DISH THEY ARE SERVED WITH A VERY SIMPLE, BUT DELICIOUS, FRESH TOMATO SAUCE.

SERVES FOUR

INGREDIENTS
675g/1½lb floury potatoes
2 egg yolks
75g/3oz/¾ cup plain (all-purpose) flour
60ml/4 tbsp finely chopped fresh
    parsley, to garnish
For the sauce
25g/1oz/2 tbsp butter, melted
450g/1lb plum tomatoes, peeled,
    seeded and chopped
salt

1 Preheat the oven to 200°C/400°F/ Gas 6. Scrub the potatoes, then bake them in their skins in the oven for 1 hour, or until the flesh feels soft when pricked with a fork.

2 While the potatoes are still warm, cut them in half and gently squeeze the flesh into a bowl, or use a spoon to scrape the flesh out of the shells. Mash the potato well, then season with a little salt. Add the egg yolks and mix lightly with a fork or spoon.

3 Add the flour and mix to a coarse dough. Place on a floured work surface and knead for 5 minutes, until the dough is smooth and elastic.

4 Shape the dough into thumb-sized shapes by making long rolls and cutting them into segments. Press each of these with the back of a fork. Place the gnocchi on a floured work surface.

5 Preheat the oven to 140°C/275°F/ Gas 1. Cook the gnocchi, in small batches, in barely simmering, slightly salted water for about 10 minutes. Remove with a slotted spoon, drain well and put in a serving dish. Cover and keep hot in the oven.

6 To make the sauce, heat the butter in a small pan for 1 minute, then add the tomatoes and cook over a low heat until the juice starts to run. Sprinkle the gnocchi with chopped parsley and serve with the sauce.

Per portion: Energy 278Kcal/1174kJ; Protein 6.9g; Carbohydrate 45.3g, of which sugars 6g; Fat 9g, of which saturates 4.4g; Cholesterol 114mg; Calcium 57mg; Fibre 3.4g; Sodium 72mg.

RISOTTO <u>WITH</u> FOUR CHEESES

THIS IS A VERY RICH DISH. IT IS THE PERFECT CHOICE FOR A DINNER PARTY WITH AN ITALIAN THEME, SERVED WITH A LIGHT, DRY SPARKLING WHITE WINE.

SERVES FOUR

INGREDIENTS
40g/1½oz/3 tbsp butter
1 small onion, finely chopped
1.2 litres/2 pints/5 cups vegetable
   stock, preferably home-made
350g/12oz/1¾ cups risotto rice
200ml/7fl oz/scant 1 cup dry
   white wine
50g/2oz/½ cup grated Gruyère cheese
50g/2oz/½ cup diced Taleggio cheese
50g/2oz/½ cup diced
   Gorgonzola cheese
50g/2oz/⅔ cup freshly grated
   Parmesan cheese
salt and ground black pepper
chopped fresh flat leaf parsley,
   to garnish

1 Melt the butter in a large, heavy pan or deep frying pan and cook the onion over a low heat, stirring frequently, for about 4–5 minutes, until softened and lightly browned. Meanwhile, pour the stock into another pan and heat it to simmering point.

2 Add the rice to the onion mixture, stir until the grains start to swell and burst, then add the wine. Stir until it stops sizzling and most of it has been absorbed by the rice, then pour in a little of the hot stock. Add salt and pepper to taste. Stir over a low heat until the stock has been absorbed.

3 Gradually add the remaining stock, a little at a time, allowing the rice to absorb the liquid before adding more, and stirring constantly. After about 20–25 minutes the rice will be *al dente* and the risotto creamy.

4 Turn off the heat under the pan, then add the Gruyère, Taleggio, Gorgonzola and 30ml/2 tbsp of the Parmesan cheese. Stir gently until the cheeses have melted, then taste and adjust the seasoning, if necessary. Spoon the risotto into a warm serving bowl and garnish with parsley. Serve immediately, handing the remaining grated Parmesan separately.

Per portion: Energy 640Kcal/2662kJ; Protein 22.1g; Carbohydrate 67.1g, of which sugars 1.2g; Fat 26g, of which saturates 15.9g; Cholesterol 70mg; Calcium 451mg; Fibre 0.2g; Sodium 473mg.

RISOTTO WITH RICOTTA AND BASIL

THIS IS A WELL-FLAVOURED RISOTTO, WHICH BENEFITS FROM THE DISTINCTIVE PUNGENCY OF BASIL, MELLOWED WITH SMOOTH RICOTTA.

SERVES THREE TO FOUR

INGREDIENTS
  45ml/3 tbsp olive oil
  1 onion, finely chopped
  275g/10oz/1½ cups risotto rice
  1 litre/1¾ pints/4 cups hot vegetable
    stock
  175g/6oz/¾ cup ricotta cheese
  50g/2oz/2 cups fresh basil leaves,
    finely chopped, plus extra
    to garnish
  75g/3oz/1 cup freshly grated
    Parmesan cheese
  salt and ground black pepper

1 Heat the oil in a large pan or flameproof casserole and cook the onion over a low heat until soft.

2 Add the rice. Cook for a few minutes, stirring constantly, until the rice grains are well coated with oil and are slightly translucent.

3 Pour in about a quarter of the stock. Cook, stirring, until all the stock has been absorbed, then add another ladleful. Continue in this manner, adding more stock when the previous ladleful has been absorbed, until the risotto has been cooking for about 20 minutes and the rice is just tender.

4 Spoon the ricotta into a bowl and break it up a little with a fork. Gently stir it into the risotto along with the chopped basil and grated Parmesan. Taste and adjust the seasoning, if necessary, then cover and leave to stand for 2–3 minutes before serving, garnished with basil leaves.

Per portion: Energy 715Kcal/2975kJ; Protein 22.4g; Carbohydrate 72.6g, of which sugars 2.8g; Fat 36.2g, of which saturates 16.4g; Cholesterol 70mg; Calcium 382mg; Fibre 0.7g; Sodium 442mg.

INDIAN MEE GORENG

*THIS IS A TRULY INTERNATIONAL DISH COMBINING INDIAN, CHINESE AND WESTERN INGREDIENTS.
IT IS A DELICIOUS TREAT FOR LUNCH OR SUPPER AND IN SINGAPORE AND MALAYSIA CAN BE
BOUGHT IN MANY STREETS FROM THE NUMEROUS HAWKERS' STALLS.*

2 If using fried tofu, cut each cube in half, refresh it in a pan of boiling water, then drain well. Heat 30ml/2 tbsp of the oil in a large frying pan. If using plain tofu, cut it into cubes and cook until brown, then lift it out with a slotted spoon and set aside.

3 Beat the eggs with the water and seasoning. Add to the oil in the frying pan and cook without stirring until set. Flip over, cook the other side, then slide it out of the pan, roll up and slice thinly.

4 Heat the remaining oil in a wok and cook the onion and garlic for 2–3 minutes. Add the drained noodles, soy sauce, ketchup and chilli sauce. Toss well over medium heat for 2 minutes, then add the diced potato. Reserve a few spring onions for garnish and stir the rest into the noodles with the chilli, if using, and the tofu.

5 When hot, stir in the omelette. Serve on a hot platter, garnished with the remaining spring onion.

SERVES FOUR TO SIX

INGREDIENTS

    450g/1lb fresh yellow egg noodles
    60–90ml/4–6 tbsp vegetable oil
    115g/4oz fried tofu or 150g/5oz
      firm tofu
    2 eggs
    30ml/2 tbsp water
    1 onion, sliced
    1 garlic clove, crushed
    15ml/1 tbsp light soy sauce
    30–45ml/2–3 tbsp tomato ketchup
    15ml/1 tbsp chilli sauce (or to taste)
    1 large cooked potato, diced
    4 spring onions (scallions), shredded
    1–2 fresh green chillies, seeded
      and thinly sliced (optional)

1 Bring a large pan of water to the boil, add the fresh egg noodles and cook for just 2 minutes. Drain the noodles and immediately rinse them under cold water to halt cooking. Drain again and set aside.

Per portion: Energy 662Kcal/2788kJ; Protein 20.7g; Carbohydrate 95.8g, of which sugars 8.8g; Fat 24.5g, of which saturates 4.9g; Cholesterol 129mg; Calcium 210mg; Fibre 4.5g; Sodium 715mg.

MUSHROOM PILAFF

THIS DISH IS SIMPLICITY ITSELF, YET IT IS FULL OF DELICIOUS INDIAN FLAVOURS.

SERVES FOUR

INGREDIENTS
- 30ml/2 tbsp vegetable oil
- 2 shallots, finely chopped
- 1 garlic clove, crushed
- 3 green cardamom pods
- 25g/1oz/2 tbsp ghee or butter
- 175g/6oz/2½ cups button (white) mushrooms, sliced
- 225g/8oz/generous 1 cup basmati rice, soaked
- 5ml/1 tsp grated fresh root ginger
- good pinch of garam masala
- 15ml/1 tbsp chopped fresh coriander (cilantro)
- salt

1 Heat the oil in a flameproof casserole and cook the shallots, garlic and cardamom pods over a medium heat for 3–4 minutes, until the shallots have softened and are beginning to brown.

2 Add the ghee or butter. When it has melted, add the mushrooms and cook for 2–3 minutes more.

3 Add the rice, ginger and garam masala. Stir-fry over a low heat for 2–3 minutes, then stir in 450ml/¾ pint/ scant 2 cups water and a little salt. Bring to the boil, then cover tightly and simmer over a low heat for 10 minutes.

4 Remove the casserole from the heat. Leave to stand, still covered, for 5 minutes. Add the chopped coriander and gently fork it through the rice. Spoon into a warm serving bowl and serve immediately.

Per portion: Energy 309Kcal/1286kJ; Protein 5.2g; Carbohydrate 46.3g, of which sugars 1g; Fat 11.2g, of which saturates 4g; Cholesterol 13mg; Calcium 18mg; Fibre 0.7g; Sodium 41mg.

ROASTED RATATOUILLE MOUSSAKA

Based on the classic Greek dish, this moussaka really has a taste of the Mediterranean. Roasting brings out the deep rich flavours of the vegetables, which give a colourful contrast to the light and mouthwatering egg-and-cheese topping. This dish is perfect as a vegetarian main course, although it may be served as a hearty winter side dish, too.

SERVES FOUR TO SIX

INGREDIENTS
2 red (bell) peppers, seeded and cut into large chunks
2 yellow (bell) peppers, seeded and cut into large chunks
2 aubergines (eggplants), cut into large chunks
3 courgettes (zucchini), thickly sliced
45ml/3 tbsp olive oil
3 garlic cloves, crushed
400g/14oz can chopped tomatoes
30ml/2 tbsp sun-dried tomato paste
45ml/3 tbsp chopped fresh basil or 15ml/1 tbsp dried basil
15ml/1 tbsp balsamic vinegar
1.5ml/¼ tsp soft light brown sugar
salt and ground black pepper
basil leaves, to garnish
For the topping
25g/1oz/2 tbsp butter
25g/1oz/¼ cup plain (all-purpose) flour
300ml/½ pint/1¼ cups milk
1.5ml/¼ tsp freshly grated nutmeg
250g/9oz ricotta cheese
3 eggs, beaten
25g/1oz/⅓ cup freshly grated Parmesan cheese

2 Mix together the oil and crushed garlic cloves and pour them over the vegetables. Shake the roasting pan to thoroughly coat the vegetables in the garlic mixture.

3 Roast in the oven for 15–20 minutes, until slightly charred, lightly tossing the vegetables once during the cooking time. Remove the pan from the oven and set aside. Reduce the oven temperature to 200°C/400°F/Gas 6.

4 Put the chopped tomatoes, sun-dried tomato paste, basil, balsamic vinegar and brown sugar in a large, heavy pan and gently heat to boiling point. Reduce the heat and simmer, uncovered, for about 10–15 minutes, until reduced and thickened, stirring occasionally. Season with salt and freshly ground black pepper to taste.

5 Carefully turn the roasted vegetables out of their pan and into the pan of tomato sauce. Mix well, coating the vegetables thoroughly in the tomato sauce. Spoon into an ovenproof dish.

6 To make the topping, melt the butter in a large, heavy pan over a gentle heat. Stir in the flour and cook for 1 minute. Pour in the milk, stirring constantly, then whisk until blended. Add the nutmeg and continue whisking over a gentle heat until thickened. Cook for a further 2 minutes, then remove from the heat and leave to cool slightly.

7 Mix in the ricotta cheese and beaten eggs thoroughly. Season with salt and plenty of freshly ground black pepper to taste.

8 Level the surface of the roasted vegetable mixture with the back of a spoon. Spoon the moussaka topping over the vegetables and sprinkle with the Parmesan cheese. Bake for 30–35 minutes, until the topping is golden brown. Serve immediately, garnished with basil leaves.

VARIATION
Rather than baking this recipe in one large dish, divide the roasted vegetables and topping among individual gratin dishes. Reduce the baking time to 25 minutes. Individual portions can also be frozen and, when needed, simply removed from the freezer, left to thaw and baked for 30–35 minutes – ideal for those with a solitary vegetarian in the family, or for unexpected guests.

1 Preheat the oven to 230°C/450°F/Gas 8. Arrange the chunks of red and yellow peppers, aubergines and courgettes in an even layer in a large roasting pan. Season well with salt and ground black pepper.

Per portion: Energy 570Kcal/2367kJ; Protein 22.1g; Carbohydrate 27.5g, of which sugars 21.7g; Fat 42.1g, of which saturates 20.3g; Cholesterol 223mg; Calcium 339mg; Fibre 7.1g; Sodium 447mg.

FIORENTINA PIZZA

AN EGG ADDS THE FINISHING TOUCH TO THIS SPINACH PIZZA; TRY NOT TO OVERCOOK IT THOUGH, AS IT'S BEST WHEN THE YOLK IS STILL SLIGHTLY SOFT IN THE MIDDLE.

SERVES TWO TO THREE

INGREDIENTS
   45ml/3 tbsp olive oil
   1 small red onion, thinly sliced
   175g/6oz fresh spinach,
     stalks removed
   1 pizza base, about
     25–30cm/10–12in diameter
   1 small jar pizza sauce
   freshly grated nutmeg
   150g/5oz mozzarella cheese
   1 egg
   25g/1oz/¼ cup grated Gruyère cheese

1 Heat 15ml/1 tbsp of the oil and cook the onion until soft. Add the spinach and cook until wilted. Drain any liquid.

2 Preheat the oven to 220°C/425°F/ Gas 7. Brush the pizza base with half the remaining olive oil. Spread the pizza sauce evenly over the base, using the back of a spoon, then top with the spinach mixture. Sprinkle over a little freshly grated nutmeg.

3 Thinly slice the mozzarella and arrange over the spinach. Drizzle over the remaining oil. Bake for 10 minutes, then remove from the oven.

4 Make a small well in the centre of the pizza topping and carefully break the egg into the hole.

5 Sprinkle over the grated Gruyère cheese and return to the oven for a further 5–10 minutes, until crisp and golden. Serve immediately.

VARIATION
Italians make a folded pizza called calzone. It is made in the same way as a pizza but is folded in half to conceal the filling. Add the egg with the rest of the pizza topping, fold over the dough, seal the edges and bake for 20 minutes.

Per portion: Energy 808Kcal/3377kJ; Protein 33.1g; Carbohydrate 72g, of which sugars 10.3g; Fat 44.8g, of which saturates 16.3g; Cholesterol 151mg; Calcium 640mg; Fibre 5.3g; Sodium 911mg.

CLASSIC MARINARA PIZZA

THE COMBINATION OF SIMPLE INGREDIENTS, FRESH GARLIC, GOOD QUALITY OLIVE OIL AND A TASTY TOMATO SAUCE GIVES THIS PIZZA AN UNMISTAKABLY ITALIAN FLAVOUR. ALTHOUGH PLAIN IN LOOKS, THE TASTE OF THE MARINARA IS UTTERLY DELICIOUS.

SERVES TWO

INGREDIENTS
   60ml/4 tbsp extra virgin olive oil or
      sunflower oil
   675g/1½lb plum tomatoes, peeled,
      seeded and chopped
   4 garlic cloves, cut into slivers
   15ml/1 tbsp chopped
      fresh oregano
   salt and ground black pepper
For the pizza base
   225g/8oz/2 cups plain (all-purpose)
      white flour
   pinch of salt
   10ml/2 tsp baking powder
   50g/2oz/4 tbsp margarine
   about 150ml/¼ pint/⅔ cup milk

1 Preheat the oven to 220ºC/425ºF/ Gas 7. Use non-stick baking parchment to line a baking sheet. Sift the flour, salt and baking powder in a bowl and rub the margarine lightly into the flour until it resembles breadcrumbs.

2 Pour in enough milk to form a soft dough and knead. Roll the dough out to a round about 25cm/10in in diameter.

3 Place the dough on the prepared baking sheet and make the edges slightly thicker than the centre.

4 Heat 30ml/2 tbsp of the oil in a pan. Add the seeded and chopped plum tomatoes and cook, stirring frequently for about 5 minutes, until soft.

5 Place the tomatoes in a sieve over a bowl and leave to drain for about 5 minutes.

6 Empty the juice from the bowl and force the tomatoes through the sieve into the bowl with the back of a spoon. You may also use a food processor or blender and process until smooth.

7 Brush the pizza base with half the remaining oil. Spoon over the tomatoes and sprinkle with garlic and oregano. Drizzle over the remaining oil and season with salt and pepper.

8 Bake for 15–20 minutes, until the pizza is crisp and golden. Serve immediately, while piping hot.

Per portion: Energy 858Kcal/3597kJ; Protein 15.6g; Carbohydrate 101.7g, of which sugars 16g; Fat 46.2g, of which saturates 4.5g; Cholesterol 4mg; Calcium 272mg; Fibre 6.9g; Sodium 266mg.

CHEESE AND ONION FLAN

THE USE OF YEAST DOUGHS FOR TARTS AND FLANS IS POPULAR IN VARIOUS REGIONS OF FRANCE. CHOOSE A STRONG CHEESE SUCH AS LIVAROT, MUNSTER OR PORT SALUT IN THIS RECIPE.

SERVES FOUR

INGREDIENTS

15g/½oz/1 tbsp butter
1 onion, halved and sliced
2 eggs
250ml/8fl oz/1 cup single
  (light) cream
225g/8oz strong semi-soft
  cheese, sliced
salt and ground black pepper
salad leaves, to serve
For the yeast dough
10ml/2 tsp dried yeast
120ml/4fl oz/½ cup milk
5ml/1 tsp sugar
1 egg yolk
225g/8oz/2 cups plain (all-purpose)
  flour, plus extra for kneading
2.5ml/½ tsp salt
50g/2oz/4 tbsp butter, softened

1 To make the dough, place the yeast in a bowl. Warm the milk in a small pan until it is at body temperature and stir into the yeast with the sugar. Continue stirring until the yeast has dissolved completely. Leave the yeast mixture to stand for about 3 minutes, then beat in the egg yolk.

COOK'S TIP

If you prefer to use easy-blend (rapid-rise) yeast, omit step 1. Beat the egg yolk and milk together in a jug (pitcher). Add the dry yeast to the flour and salt in the food processor and pulse to combine. Pour in the egg and milk mixture and proceed with the recipe as normal.

2 Put the flour and salt in a food processor fitted with a metal blade and pulse to combine. With the machine running, slowly pour in the yeast mixture. Scrape down the sides and continue processing for 2–3 minutes. Add the softened butter and process for another 30 seconds.

3 Transfer the dough to a lightly greased bowl. Cover the bowl with a dishtowel and leave to rise in a warm place for about 1 hour, until the dough has doubled in bulk.

4 Remove the dough from the bowl and place on a lightly floured surface. Knock back (punch down) the dough by hitting it with your fist. Sprinkle a little more flour on the work surface and roll out the dough to a 30cm/12in round.

5 Line a 23cm/9in flan tin (quiche pan) with the dough. Gently press it into the tin and trim off any overhanging pieces, leaving a 3mm/⅛in rim around the flan case (pie shell). Cover with a dishtowel, set aside in a warm place and leave the dough to rise again for about 30 minutes, or until puffy.

6 Meanwhile, melt the butter in a heavy pan and add the onion. Cover the pan and cook over a medium-low heat, stirring occasionally, for about 15 minutes, until softened and lightly coloured. Remove the lid and continue cooking, stirring frequently, until the onion is very soft and caramelized.

7 Preheat the oven to 180°C/350°F/ Gas 4. Beat together the eggs and cream. Season and stir in the cooked onion.

8 Arrange the cheese on the base of the flan case. Pour over the egg mixture and bake for 30–35 minutes, until the base is golden and the centre is just set. Cool slightly on a wire rack and serve warm with salad leaves.

Per portion: Energy 747Kcal/3113kJ; Protein 27.1g; Carbohydrate 49.6g, of which sugars 5.9g; Fat 49.2g, of which saturates 29.9g; Cholesterol 271mg; Calcium 619mg; Fibre 2.3g; Sodium 576mg.

INDEX